I0170408

ESTHER'S MYSTERIES

Behind the Mask

A BEKY Book ©

Hollisa Alewine

CONTENTS

GLOSSARY

Achashverosh - Ahaseurus, possibly the historical Xerxes

Adonai – my Lord.

HaBrit HaChadasha – New Testament. In Hebrew, literally, "Renewed Covenant." The Hebrew word for new, chadash, also means renewed, as we apply the adjective to the New Moon. The moon is not new; it is the same moon. Its appearance is merely renewed each month. By the same token, Jeremiah 31:31 defines the terms of the New Covenant: the Torah will be written on the hearts of God's people. It is not a new Torah, but the old Torah renewed in a dynamic way because of the work of Yeshua, a better mediator than Moses.

Chag – Usually, a Biblical feast such as Passover, Shavuot, or Sukkot.

Chiastic/chiasm – A chiastic structure is a literary technique wherein a story is divided into two halves and the themes of the first half of the story are repeated in the second half of the story in reverse order. Furthermore, the two halves of the chiastic structure "point" to the most important element of the structure, the central axis. *This is illustrated below, where "C" is the axis:*

A. Daniel 2: Four Gentile world empires
    B. Daniel 3: Gentile persecution of Israel
        C. Daniel 4: Divine providence over Gentiles
        C'. Daniel 5: Divine providence over Gentiles
    B'. Daniel 6: Gentile persecution of Israel
A'. Daniel 7: Four Gentile world empires

Here is an example from the Book of Revelation by

chapter, contributed by Mariela Perez-Rosas, with "G" as the axis: [1]

A 1 Prologue and greeting: Alef-Tav[1]; He who comes
  B 2-3 Seven Assemblies
    C 4-5 Celestial Vision
      D 6-8 Seven Seals, Seven Trumpets
        E 7 The Sealed
          F 10-11 Angel, 2 Witnesses
            G 12 The Woman-Male Son-Dragon
          F 13 Dragon, 2 Beasts
        E 14 The New Song
      D 15-18 Seven Plagues, Seven Cups
    C 19-20 Celestial Vision
  B 21 New Jerusalem
A 22 Epilogue and farewell: Alef-Tav; He who comes

For an easy exercise in understanding chiastic structure, cut out the graphic of the menorah in the Appendix. Fold the menorah along its axis, the middle branch of Weeks. The first and last branches will become "mirrors" of one another, as will the second and sixth branches and the third and fifth branches.

Elohim – God the Creator.

Hermeneutics – Methods of Biblical interpretation applying accepted rules of interpretation.

Mashiach - Messiah, the Anointed One

Megillah - scroll

Menorah – a lampstand, specifically, the seven-branched golden lampstand that stood in the Holy Place of the Tabernacle and Temple.

Metaphor – a thing regarded as representative or symbolic of something else, especially something abstract.

1. Alpha and Omega in Greek.

Mitzvah – Commandment

Moed(im) - alludes to seasons and the appointed feasts of Israel: Passover, Unleavened Bread, Firstfruits of the Barley, Firstfruits of the Wheat (Pentecost), Trumpets, Day of Atonement, and Tabernacles

Nedar - Vow. Plural is nedarim.

Pur - lots, objects of gambling or chance; plural is purim.

Ruach HaKodesh – Holy Spirit.

Shabbat – Shabbat starts at sundown on Friday evenings and extends to sundown on Saturday, the seventh day.

Sukkah/sukkot – a covered booth or tabernacle

Tallit - a prayer shawl with four cords of blue affixed to its corners.

TANAKH – Old Testament. Tanakh is an acronym for Torah, Neviim, Ketuvim, or Law, Prophets, and Writings, the ancient divisions of the Hebrew Bible. The books of the Tanakh are the same as, but are not arranged in the same order as Christian Bibles.

Torah – The first five books of the Bible, misunderstood as "law" in English translations. The Torah is more accurately God's teaching and instruction. It contains topics such as science, history, priestly procedures, civil statutes, ordinances, health, agriculture, commandments, prophecies, prayer, animal husbandry, architecture, civics, and many others. The root word of Torah comes from the Hebrew word *yarah*, which means "to hit the mark." Torah may also be used to refer to all of the Hebrew Bible, or even to its smallest meaning, a procedure. Torah may be used by Messianic Jews to refer to the entire Bible from Genesis to Revelation, for the Torah is the foundation for all the Scriptures. The Prophets point Israel back to the Torah. The Psalms teach one to love the Torah as King David loved it. The Writings teach the consequences of departing from the Torah and the rewards for returning to it. The New Testament brings the Torah to its fullest meaning in the person Yeshua the Messiah, and much of the New Testament quotes the Tanakh.

Yeshua – Jesus' Hebrew name; salvation.

1

PENNING PATTERNS

The foundational books of Scripture are the five books of the Bible, or Pentateuch. These five books, the Torah, contain wonderful prophecies; however, many of them are not obvious. They are concealed and covered, and the nuances of the events are not revealed until later in the Scriptures. This is a wonder to consider. The Torah[2] was not given to Moses through dreams, visions, or dark sayings. They were given to him directly. These five books are the plainest of prophecies! Most prophecy conferences don't begin in the Torah, but the books of the prophets and Revelation.

Regardless, prophecies form a pattern in Scripture, and the pattern is a recurrence of themes. Understanding that the patterns are there is the first step to understanding that Biblical prophecy repeats itself. Don't ask, "When will this prophecy be fulfilled?" Instead ask, "How many times will it be fulfilled?" Esther's prophecies behind the veil will find their first cycles in the books of the Torah, primarily in Genesis.

The Creation in Genesis is the seed form of the succeeding prophecies of the Bible. The specific actions taken in Days 1-7 continue to unfold in a

2. For a simple overview of the definition of "Torah," see BEKY Booklet *What is the Torah?* by the author.

cycle of fulfillments. The many narratives in the Torah give us a glimpse of at least a portion of the prophetic cycle. One example is the crossing of the Reed Sea, which reflects Days One through Four of Creation:

> Day One: Light is separated from darkness. The Israelites are led from Egypt, and a pillar of fire separates them from their enemies. There was even a plague in which the Hebrews had "light in all their dwellings" but the Egyptians suffered from a tangible darkness.
>
> Day Two: The waters are separated from the waters. The waters are separated and piled up so that the Israelites can take the third step...
>
> Day Three: Dry land appears. The Israelites walk across on dry land. On Day Three of Creation, trees appear as well as springs and rivers in the "gathering" of the waters. At Marah, Moses sweetens a gathering of bitter waters by throwing in a stick, which is an *etz* (tree), in Hebrew.
>
> Day Four: Sun, moon, and stars appear for the *moedi*[3]. Moses leads the Hebrews toward Mount Sinai, where they will receive instructions concerning the appointed times of their calendar.

3. The calendar and feast days of Passover, Unleavened Bread, Firstfruits of Barley and Wheat (Weeks), Trumpets, Atonements, and Tabernacles, also the seasons. Hebrew feast days are set within a particular season, not migrating through the year as some lunar-based calendars.

4. There is a lectionary of the Torah and Prophets that is read in synagogues on a weekly basis, so the entire Torah is covered in one year. Some congregations follow a triennial schedule, which allows study of smaller portions.

The prophetic pattern extends beyond Day Four, but the preceding example demonstrates how the pattern works. It's possible to find evidence of this Genesis pattern throughout the Torah. There are also concepts presented in an earlier weekly Torah portion[4] that will apply to later ones. The patterns in the first five books of the Bible, the Torah, are penned in succeeding books of the Bible as well, including *HaBrit HaChadasha*. [5]   Part of understanding prophecy is identifying a pattern of connected events. Rabbi David Fohrman writes:

> When in one story, the Bible repeatedly quotes from an earlier Biblical narrative, the text is conveying something profound to the reader. The Bible is creating its own internal commentary on the meaning of its text. It is saying, 'if you really want to understand what is going on over here, you need first to understand what's going on over there. You need to see the second story in light of the first.' (Fohrman, 2011)

The Torah narrative of Joseph's life is an example of internal commentary. There are very specific events, places, objects, themes, and attitudes in the Genesis story of Joseph that apply to Messiah Yeshua.[6] In fact, Messianic understanding in rabbinic literature includes *Mashiach ben Yosef* (Messiah Son of Joseph), a Messiah who will suffer for his people. The Gospels focus on this aspect of Messiah and not so much on his identity as *Mashiach ben David*, the conquering king as portrayed in Revelation. The suffering servant Joseph and King David types and shadows both appear in the Scroll of Esther, a book full of prophecy. This is one line of investigation to pursue.

Another line of investigation includes a section of Torah called *Nedarim*, or Vows. Vows in the Torah are connected with the *chagim*,[7] but they are obscure in practicality today. There is no Temple in which an Israelite could pay his vows, nor a functional priesthood to receive them. In spite of the practicality of such prophecy in the Torah, there

5. The New Testament, The New Covenant

6. Jesus Christ

7. *Moedim*, or feast days. Nahum One urges Judah to perform his vows in connection with keeping the *chagim*. The chagim are the three "foot festivals" of Passover, Weeks, and Tabernacles. The moedim are generally Passover, Unleavened Bread, First Fruits of Barley, Weeks, Trumpets, Atonements, and Tabernacles.

is a thematic connection in Esther to vows and the feasts: Passover, Unleavened Bread, Firstfruits of Barley, Firstfruits of Wheat, Feast of Trumpets, The Day of Coverings, and Tabernacles.

English	Hebrew Transliteration
Passover	Pesach
Unleavened Bread	Chag HaMatzah
Firstfruits of Barley	Yom HaBikkurim
Pentecost or Weeks (Wheat)	Shavuot
Trumpets	Rosh HaShanah/Yom Teruah
Atonement, i.e., "coverings"	Yom HaKippurim
Tabernacles or Ingathering	Sukkot, Asiph

8. "The husband must fulfill his duty to his wife, and likewise also the wife to her husband. The wife does not have authority over her own body, but the husband does; and likewise, also the husband does not have authority over his own body, but the wife does. Stop depriving one another, except by agreement for a time, so that you may devote yourselves to prayer, and come together again so that Satan will not tempt you because of your lack of self-control."
I Co 7:3-6

Prophecy is given greater scope as it develops in Scripture, expanding understanding of the foundational Torah with the help of the internal commentaries. For example, sometimes the Scriptures give instructions that seem to apply only in a specific area or to a specific person, but later the application is enlarged. One area is specific responsibilities given to the Israelite male or husband. The husband is given the primary responsibility to provide food, shelter, and conjugal rights to his wife. Those are irreducible obligations to a healthy man.

On the other hand, Proverbs Thirty-one, even though a parable of the Holy Spirit, describes a woman who helps meet two of those three family needs. Concerning the third, conjugal rights, although the husband is given primary responsibility, Paul states that women also bear the responsibility; Paul says that the woman does not have the authority of her own body, but the man, and the man does not have the authority of his own body, but the woman. Paul says neither should abstain from that responsibility unless it is by mutual agreement for a specific purpose of fasting and prayer.[8]

Men are the primary prophets and evangelists in

Israel, yet the role is also filled by Miriam, Huldah, Deborah, Phillip's seven daughters, the women in Acts Two, and others. Paul gives the Corinthians instructions for women who prophesy within the local congregation. The question is not *will they* speak up to prophesy, but *how they* should do it.

Men go through a selection process to be fit for war, yet Deborah is summoned by Barak in the Book of Judges to lead the Israelite army. Judges in Israel have criteria that apply specifically to men, yet Deborah functions in that role of interpreting and applying Torah for pre-monarchal Israel. Men are given the primary responsibility for attending the three pilgrimage feasts, yet it is evident through Scripture that entire families would attend and celebrate. This is how Yeshua managed to attend a Scriptural discussion with top scholars in the Temple at about the age of twelve, giving both his father and mother a scare. These are only a few of the mirror patterns, but Esther will add perhaps the most beautiful of them all.

Esther's scroll is full of similar prophetic internal commentaries. Esther explains how the male/female roles function in obedience to the Holy Spirit in order. Husbands and fathers are given the responsibility for the validation of a woman's vow in Numbers 30:1-16. However, in the Scroll of Esther, that role is reversed, or more accurately, expanded. In fact, Esther faces death if she fails to fulfill…or perhaps share…the "male" role.

Why are so many of these gems veiled throughout the Scripture? There are at least 70 answers, but one answer is the mystery of the Gentiles. When women are involved, Israel's tent is enlarged.

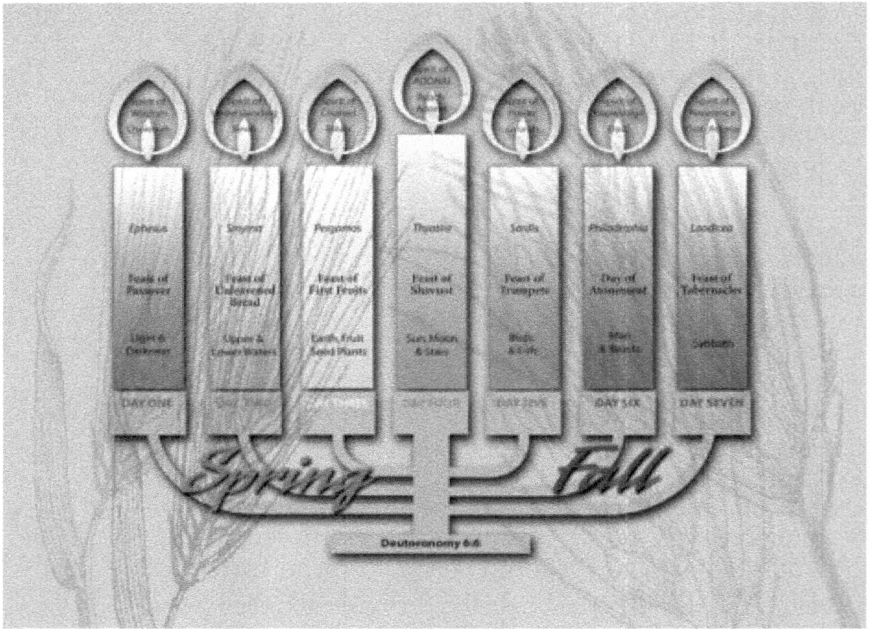

Figure 1

14

2

THE COVER-UP

One of the first Torah clues in the investigation into Esther's secrets is actually a failure. This failure involved a Gentile's attempt to join the family of Israel. Dinah was both a daughter and sister of Israel. She was raped by a Gentile prince, Shechem, but he'd apparently repented[9] of his sin and wanted to make it right by marrying her. Instead, Dinah's brothers Shimon and Levi slaughtered the Shechemites, something made possible by duping them into keeping a commandment, the circumcision.

> Then Jacob said to Simeon and Levi,
> 'You have brought trouble on me
> by making me odious among the
> inhabitants of the land, among the
> Canaanites and the Perizzites; and
> my men being few in number, they
> will gather together against me and
> attack me and I will be destroyed,
> I and my household.' But they
> said, '*Should he treat our sister as a
> harlot?*' (Ge 34:30-31)

9. The repentance may be called in question since Shechem does not release Dinah back to her family. Negotiation under duress is not free negotiation.

Although the two brothers effectively blocked the Gentiles from joining Israel's household, the hint is given by Shimon and Levi. That hint is a thread present throughout the Torah, the Prophets, the Writings, and the New Covenant. The thread will be the clouded issue of a woman's character:

- Sister or harlot?
- Virtuous woman or prostitute?
- Faithful wife or adulteress?

Dinah was a virgin, but she was treated as a harlot. This is a part of the hint. It is the motivations of men being exposed by the question of Dinah's character. In the Scroll of Esther, there is a similar question hidden in a tiny grammatical ambiguity. To this day, those celebrating Purim[10] wear masks or costumes, concealing their true identity. All the way from the Torah to the Gospels, women both conceal and reveal righteousness. Even Mary Magdalene, the first witness of the resurrection, is often portrayed as a loose woman without any real textual evidence. Since she had been delivered of seven spirits, it is *assumed* she was a woman of bad character.

Esther is a woman functioning in a hidden role. In fact, those celebrating her Feast of Purim[11] are characterized wearing masks or costumes, concealing their true identity. Hadassah is Esther's Hebrew name. The Persian king searched for a replacement for Queen Vashti. When she is selected by King Achashverosh's[12] messengers to become part of his harem, she is Esther. Esther is "star" in Persian, but "secret" in Hebrew. Hadassah's cousin Mordechai, who took care of her after she was orphaned, cautioned her to conceal her identity. This she did.

Although Esther puts on the mask of a Persian name, her Hebrew name is Hadassah, which means a myrtle tree. Myrtle is one of the leafy branches that is waved toward the four corners of the earth with the *lulav*[13] during the Feast of Sukkot. Esther's very name hints at Sukkot,[14] and her status as an orphan and an alien in Persian exile also hint to Sukkot.

Sukkot is an appointed time to welcome and do good to the stranger, alien, orphan, and widow. The 70 years of exile in Babylon[15] allotted to Judah also allude to Sukkot, the Feast of the Nations, when 70 bulls were offered at the Temple during the *moed*. Seventy is a number that represents the nations. Israel went down to Egypt 70 in number, and the nations were divided according to that number.[16]

Just as Hadassah concealed her Jewish identity from the king, the Fall Feasts are themed with coverings (Yom HaKippurim, the Day of Coverings), the clouds of the Feast of Trumpets, and even the *sukkah* [17] of Sukkot is a covering.[18] Her husband King Achashverosh doesn't know who Queen Esther is until the Day of Trouble! In order to compare other situations of mistaken or questionable identities, turn to the Torah to establish context. Let's construct some questions to guide our thinking:

- Who are "These"?
- Who is Esther?
- Who are the other matriarchs and heroines of Scripture? What is the pattern of their thinking and actions?
- Does Esther fit this pattern?
- What is their ultimate goal in concealing their identities?
- Who will benefit?

Let's start with the question, "Who are these?"

15. Figuratively the nations, for Babylon (Babel) was the location from which the nations and tongues were scattered

16. Ex 1:5; Dt 32:8

17. A three-sided temporary shelter roofed with branches and decorated with fruits and other produce

18. See *Creation Gospel Workbook One*

3

KAIN WASN'T ABEL

As early as the story of Kain and Abel, the cycle of prophecy is illustrated. The two boys each bring a gift to the altar *miketz yamim* "at the end of days," a prophecy.[19] Their gifts suggest those that Israel brought to the Feast of Tabernacles, or Sukkot, which was the year-end of the festivals. These festivals, even when celebrated as more of a proto-type by Kain and Abel, are part of the pattern of prophecy. By bringing the choicest of his flock, Abel prophesied of an ingathering at the end of days. Who these sheep are, however, may sometimes be a mystery to the Biblical figures:

> *(Esau to Jacob)* He lifted his eyes and saw the women and the children, and said, '*Who are these* with you?' So he said, 'The *children whom God has graciously given* your servant.' (Ge 33:5)

> *(Jacob to Joseph)* When Israel saw Joseph's sons, he said, '*Who are these*?' Joseph said to his father, 'They are *my sons, whom God has given me* here.' So he said, 'Bring them to me, please, that I may *bless*

19. Ge 4:3 The Hebrew has different English translations, less literal, such as "in the course of time."

them.' (Ge 48:8-9)

(The Holy One to Rachel) The
children of whom you were
bereaved [in exile] will yet say in your
ears, 'The place is too cramped for
me; make room for me that I may
live here.' Then you will say in your
heart, *'Who has begotten these* for
me, since I have been *bereaved*
of my children and am *barren, an*
exile and a wanderer? And *who*
has reared these? Behold, I was
left alone; *from where did these*
come?'" Thus says the Lord GOD,
'Behold, I will lift up My hand to the
nations and set up My standard
to *the peoples;* and they will bring
your sons in their bosom, and your
daughters will be carried on their
shoulders.' (Is 49:20-22)

(The Holy One to Israel and
Jerusalem) Who are these who fly
like a cloud and like the doves to
their lattices? Surely the coastlands
will wait for Me; and the ships of
Tarshish will come first, to bring *your*
sons from afar, their silver and their
gold with them, for the name of
the LORD your God, and for the
Holy One of Israel because He has
glorified you. (Is 60:8-9)

Here is a summary of "These," which will eventually
yield that internal commentary on the Scroll of Esther
and solve the question of who she is. "These" are:

- Women and children
- Exiles from Israel and Jerusalem
- Gift of God
- Joseph's sons (born in Egypt/nations)

- Blessing
- Missing children
- Children of a barren, exiled, wandering woman left alone
- Concealed and reared among the nations to fly home like returning doves
- Returned home by the nations
- Accompanied by silver and gold

Here are more hints from an associated theme in Genesis 48, shepherds:

> And he blessed Joseph and said, 'The God before whom my fathers Abraham and Isaac walked, *the God who has been my shepherd all my life long to this day*, the angel who has redeemed me from all evil, *bless the boys*; and in them let my name be carried on, and the name of my fathers Abraham and Isaac; and *let them grow into a multitude in the midst of the earth.*' (Ge 48:15-16)

Even in giving this blessing to his grandsons, Jacob appears confused to Joseph:

> When Joseph saw that his father laid his right hand on the head of Ephraim, it displeased him, and he took his father's hand to move it from Ephraim's head to Manasseh's head. And Joseph said to his father, 'Not this way, my father; since this one is the firstborn, put your right hand on his head.'
>
> But his father refused and said, 'I know, my son, I know. He also shall become a people, and he also shall be great. Nevertheless, his younger

20. Also see
Genesis 49:24

21. The Rule of
First Mention is
allowing the first
mention of a
word or concept
in Scripture to
establish its
fundamental
meaning. By
referencing
Genesis One,
we are using
the Rule of First
Mention to
establish the
significance of
concepts such
as darkness,
light, water, sun,
moon, stars,
birds, fish, man,
etc. Another
rule is the Rule
of Complete
Mention. In
yeshiva, it is
known as Hillel's
7th Rule of
Interpretation:
*Davar hilmad
me'anino*
(Explanation
obtained from
context). This rule
states that the
total context, not
just the isolated
statement, must
be considered
for an accurate
exegesis.

22. Rachel
means a female
lamb

23. See
*Creation Gospel
Workbook One*

brother shall be greater than he,
and *his offspring shall become a
multitude of nations.*' (Ge 48:17-19)

Jacob was not confused about Ephraim's identity at all! He knew exactly who "these" were. Jacob's blessing adds the shepherd[20] concept to that of the nations. Let's apply another hermeneutical tool, the Rule of First Mention.[21] Who was the first shepherd? Abel.

Although they seem unrelated, the Hebrew root of the name Joseph and who named him are important. The Hebrew root is *asaph*, meaning to add or increase in number; to ingather. Joseph's mother Rachel was a shepherdess, a formerly barren woman, and she named him, for she wanted Adonai to add to her children. Read carefully the accounts of Abel and Rachel to build the context:

* Rachel the "ewe"[22] and shepherdess in Genesis 35:15-20
* Abel the shepherd in Genesis 4:1-10

The proto-prophetic narrative of Kain and Abel describes the brothers bringing their gifts at "the end of days." In Hebrew, this is *miketz yamim*. This describes Sukkot, the last of the annual feasts, the last days of celebration. At this feast, it is appropriate to bring the first fruits of the flock *or* produce. Abel brings choice lambs from the flock, his best gift. Kain, however, brought of "*the* fruit of the ground."[23]

The commandment, however, states:

> And you shall take of *the first of
> every fruit of the ground* that you
> bring in from your Land that Hashem
> your God gives to you…You shall
> come to whomever will be the priest
> in those days and you shall say to
> him, 'I declare today…And now,

behold! I have brought the *first fruit* of the ground…' (Dt 26:1 Artscroll)

Why was it so important for Kain and Abel both to bring their best gift during the last days? Prophetically, who was to benefit from the Feast of Sukkot?   The key categories of people are named:

> You shall celebrate the Feast of Booths seven days after you have gathered in from your threshing floor and your wine vat; and you shall rejoice in your feast, *you and your son and your daughter and your male and female servants and the Levite and the stranger and the orphan and the widow who are in your towns*…LORD your God will bless you in all your produce and in all the work of your hands, so that you will be altogether joyful. (Dt 16:13-15)

> Then it will come about that *any who are left of all the nations* that went against Jerusalem will go up from year to year to worship the King, the LORD of hosts, and to celebrate the Feast of Booths. And it will be that whichever of *the families of the earth* does not go up to Jerusalem to worship the King, the LORD of hosts, there will be no rain on them. If *the family of Egypt* does not go up or enter, then no rain will fall on them; it will be the plague with which the LORD smites *the nations* who do not go up to celebrate the Feast of Booths. This will be the punishment of *Egypt*, and the punishment of *all the nations* who do not go up to celebrate the Feast of Booths. (Zech 14:16-19)

Notice a parallelism in Zechariah. Egypt's fate is equal to the fate of all the nations. Egypt is symbolic of all the nations who hid Rachel's exiled children, represented by Joseph, the son with the name linked with Sukkot. Of all the matriarchs, Rachel is buried oddly. She is buried on the road to Bethlehem. According to tradition, it is so that she will intercede for her children being marched out of Jerusalem into Babylonian exile, and so she will see them return and say, "Who are these? Where did these come from?" They might look a little more Babylonian than Israelite when they return.

Egypt was the site of the first Israelite Passover, and immediately upon leaving their exile in Egypt with the mixed multitude from other nations, the Hebrews camped at Sukkot. From Rachel's pattern in Genesis 35:15-20 some context keys appear:

- The name *Ben-Oni*, son of suffering or affliction; *ani* means poor or afflicted
- Bitter suffering
- Severe labor

All these are hints to the Passover from Egypt. Ben-Oni hints to the Bread of Affliction (*HaLachma **Ania***), which is Passover *matzah*, the unleavened bread eaten with the bitter herbs. They represent the bitter tears shed in the Egyptian slavery and exile from The Land of Promise. In spite of the affliction, the Hebrews increased. As Joseph's name prophesied, Rachel was added children:

> But the more they afflicted (*anah*) them, the more they multiplied and the more they spread out, so that they were in dread of the sons of Israel. (Ex 1:12)

Another context clue was Rachel's severe labor in childbirth. This is related to the Hebrew word often translated in English as tribulation (*tzar*), to squeeze in a narrow place. The Hebrew root of Egypt is the same, *tzar*. Egypt in Hebrew is *Mitzraim*, which can literally translate, "the means by which tribulations are accomplished" or "from tribulations." [24] Sukkot of the Nations begins at the Passover from Egypt:

> Now the sons of Israel had done according to the word of Moses, for they had *requested from the Egyptians articles of silver and articles of gold*, and clothing; and the LORD had given the people favor in the sight of the Egyptians, so that they let them have their request. Thus they plundered the Egyptians. Now the sons of Israel journeyed from Rameses to *Succot*, about six hundred thousand men on foot, aside from children. *A mixed multitude also went up with them, along with flocks and herds, a very large number of livestock.*
> (Ex 12:35-38)

Rachel and Abel picture the role of a shepherd. Rachel portrays the suffering of Passover for her lambs. Abel portrays the expectancy of the nations at Sukkot, a very large number of flocks represented by his choicest ones. If the first is holy and good, then so is the rest of the flock or field. On the menorah of the festivals, the end is declared from the Beginning. Passover is connected to Sukkot.[25] The following Jeremiah text addressed to Rachel adds more context clues:

> Hear the word of the LORD,
> *O nations*, and declare in the coastlands afar off, and say, 'He who scattered Israel will gather him and *keep him as a shepherd keeps his flock*.' For the LORD has ransomed Jacob and redeemed

24. See *Creation Gospel Workbook One*

25. Ibid.

him from the hand of him who was stronger than he. They will come and shout for joy on the height of Zion, and they will be radiant over the bounty of the LORD-- over *the grain and the new wine and the oil, and over the young of the flock and the herd; and their life will be like a watered garden*, and they will never languish again. Then the virgin will rejoice in the dance, and the young men and the old, together, for I will turn their *mourning into joy* and will comfort them and *give them joy for their sorrow*. I will fill the soul of the priests with abundance, and My people will be satisfied with My goodness,' declares the LORD.

Thus says the LORD, 'A voice is heard in Ramah, *lamentation and bitter weeping. Rachel is weeping for her children*; she refuses to be comforted for her children, *because they are no more.*' Thus says the LORD, 'Restrain your voice from weeping and your eyes from tears; for your work will be rewarded,' declares the LORD, 'And they will return from the land of the enemy. There is hope for your future,' declares the LORD, 'And *your children* will return to their own territory.' (Je 31:10-17)

In Jeremiah 31:10-17 there are several thematic context clues to the *chagim*, the three pilgrimage festivals of Pesach, Shavuot, and Sukkot.

Sukkot Context Clues:

- Nations
- A shepherd keeps and gathers his flock

- Joy
- Grain, new wine, oil
- Young of the flock and herd

Shavuot Context Clue:

- Your work will be rewarded[26]

Pesach Context Clues:

- Lamentation and bitter weeping
- Refusing comfort
- Mourning and sorrow

Most of this passage in Jeremiah could be addressed to Jacob, not Rachel, for he was the one bereaved, and it was her children who were bereaved of Rachel! When confronted with the potential loss of his youngest son Benjamin, Jacob is the one who says, "If I am bereaved, I am bereaved." *Jacob* was the stranger and a wanderer! Jeremiah is nudging us to understand both a "male" and "female" side of this prophecy.

26. The Book of Ruth is traditionally associated with and read at Shavuot. (Boaz to Ruth) "The LORD bless your work and a *full reward* be given you…"

4

SCARLET HARLOT OR ANOTHER MOTHER?

In his prophecy, Jeremiah mentions that Rachel's children are "No more." Joseph and Benjamin did live, but Joseph's brothers describe him as "no more" when they believe he is just an Egyptian viceroy, not their brother. Rachel died on the way to Ephrath,[27] and she alone among the matriarchs and patriarchs was not buried in the Cave of Machpelah. The root of Ephrath is *perat*, meaning fruit. Fruit is an offering brought at Sukkot, and one must mention the Exodus from Egypt when the fruit is offered[28] in baskets. Rachel died and was buried alone before she could reach Ephrath, the fruit of Sukkot.

The root of Joseph's name, *asaph*, is the form of another word for Sukkot, the Feast of Ingathering, *Asiph*. Rachel named her second son Ben-Oni, which suggests the suffering of Passover. Jacob, however, changes the name to Ben-Yamin, son of the Right Hand, suggesting the throne, a key symbol of Sukkot and the fall feasts. Rachel will not be comforted until her children among every nation, tribe, and tongue are returned to her in the Land. The context of Genesis 48:3-8 provides further clues:

27. Bethlehem

28. Dt 26

29

Then Jacob said to Joseph, 'God Almighty appeared to me at Luz in the land of Canaan and blessed me, and He said to me, 'Behold, I will make you fruitful and numerous, and I will *make you a company of peoples*, and will give this land to your descendants after you for an everlasting possession...' Now as for me, when I came from Paddan, *Rachel died, to my sorrow*, in the land of Canaan on the journey, when there was still some distance to go to *Ephrath*; and I buried her there on the way to Ephrath...

When Israel saw Joseph's sons, he said, *'Who are these?'* Joseph said to his father, *'They are my sons, whom God has given me here.'* So he said, 'Bring them to me, please, that *I may bless them.'* (Ge 48:3-9)

Within Jacob's conversation with Joseph is embedded a Hebrew clue: "Rachel died, *to my sorrow*, in the land of Canaan on the journey, when there was still some distance to go to Ephrath; and I buried her there on the way to Ephrath..." A hint is an unusual use of a Hebrew word for "sorrow." The word Jacob used for sorrow is *alai*, which implies Rachel died *because of* Jacob.

Sorrow = *alai* = On my account, on my behalf, because of, for the sake of...

The shepherdess Rachel suffered in bearing and losing her children for "Jacob's sake." While we could attribute Rachel's death to the curse Jacob utters on whomever has Laban's household idols,[29] it may be deeper than that. What if it was for the Promise?

29. Ge 31:32

30

> May God Almighty bless you and
> make you fruitful and multiply you,
> that you may become a company
> of peoples. (Ge 28:3)

Rachel's suffering, pictured by the Passover, was so that the Promise handed down from Abraham to Isaac to Jacob that they would become a "company of peoples" could be fulfilled in the Sukkot of the Nations prophesied by Zechariah.

> Then God said to Abraham…Sarah
> shall be her name. I will bless her,
> and indeed I will give you a son by
> her. Then I will bless her, and *she*
> *shall be a mother of nations*; kings
> of peoples will come from her.
> Then Abraham fell on his face and
> laughed, and said in his heart, 'Will a
> child be born to a man one hundred
> years old? And will Sarah, who is
> ninety years old, bear a child?' (Ge
> 17:15-17)

Sarah, Rebecca, and Rachel endured long periods of barrenness, but each conceived children of promise. The children of these three barren matriarchs are exiled and hidden among nations, like Yeshua's parable of good leaven of the Kingdom hidden in three pecks of flour.[30] These women longed to see the promise fulfilled. Prophetically, they endured Passover for Sukkot. Rachel is still weeping for her children. The shepherdess longs for her sheep to come home. What does she have in common with Abel?

> A voice that reaches to the heavens
> Untimely death, buried alone
> Lambs and shepherding
> A prophecy of Sukkot.

Abel's Sukkot offering was an act of obedience that   30. Mt 13:33

prophesied of the ingathering of the exiles even before there were nations! Kain did not keep the feast as commanded, not sharing his first fruit, his best. Every act of obedience to God's Word can be a prophecy affirming His will on Earth. Abel's blood continues to cry from the ground for the nations. Like Joseph who was "no more" because of his dreams and coat of many-colored nations, Abel was despised for his vision. Keeping the feasts of the Lord in Spirit and Truth will bring suffering before it brings reward!

So who are these? These are the missing lambs of the shepherd Abel, the missing children of Rachel in every generation. Yeshua is still looking for shepherds and shepherdesses in this generation to proclaim the gospel by worshipping Adonai at His appointed times, His feasts. The disciple Peter is an example of how Abels and Rachels today are called to seek the sheep and care for them so that Rachel can be comforted.

> This is now the *third time* that Jesus was manifested to the disciples, after He was raised from the dead. So when they had finished breakfast, Jesus said to Simon Peter, 'Simon, son of John, do you love Me more than these?'
>
> He said to Him, 'Yes, Lord; You know that I love You.'
>
> He said to him, '*Tend My lambs.*' He said to him again a second time, 'Simon, son of John, do you love Me?'
>
> He said to Him, 'Yes, Lord; You know that I love You.' He said to him, '*Shepherd My sheep.*' He said to him the *third time*, 'Simon, son of

John, do you love Me?'

Peter was grieved because He said to him the third time, 'Do you love Me?' And he said to Him, 'Lord, You know all things; You know that I love You.'

Jesus said to him, '*Tend My sheep*. Truly, truly, I say to you, when you were younger, you used to gird yourself and walk wherever you wished; but when you grow old, you will stretch out your hands and someone else will gird you, and bring you where you do not wish to go.' *Now this He said, signifying by what kind of death he would glorify God*. And when He had spoken this, He said to him, 'Follow Me!' (Jn 21:14-19)

There is a cost to live the prophetic life of Abel and Rachel. It requires the sacrifice of death, a Passover so that we, like the Lamb who was slain, can be worthy of our calling. The Promise of the Father is brought forth through tribulations. Regardless, Yeshua says, "Follow me!"

I am the good shepherd, and I know My own and My own know Me, even as the Father knows Me and I know the Father; and I lay down My life for the sheep. I have other sheep, which are not of this fold; I must bring them also, and they will hear My voice; and they will become one flock with one shepherd. *For this reason the Father loves Me, because I lay down My life* so that I may take it again. (Jn 10:14-17)

What does Queen Esther say when she agrees to go

before the King at the risk of her life to find salvation for the exiled children of Judah and Israel? "If I perish, I perish." The lambs were in jeopardy. The One who called her to the appointed time, which so happened to be during the days of Unleavened Bread, could take her life back up again should she perish in obedience to Him.

Another magnificent example of the pattern that adds the nations to Israel is the Book of Ruth, which is read at Shavuot. In summary, these points are part of the narrative:

- Widow and stranger
- Returns to the Land of Israel
- Obeys the Covenant of Israel (Torah)
- Becomes a Covenant bride in Israel and
- Produces offspring (people) in the Land and Covenant

What if Judah's offspring had never even lived to suffer the tribulations of exile in Babylon and the threat of Haman's sword? In the narrative of Tamar and Judah is a summary that includes the added Ruth clue of "widow," one of the special classes of guest at Sukkot. Another clue ties the reader back to the sister Dinah, who was treated as a "harlot":

- Tamar is a widow
- Mistaken for a temple prostitute and adulteress
- A stranger, a Canaanite

Was Tamar a virtuous woman and a mother in Israel? Her disguise was very effective at leading Judah at first to believe otherwise:

31. *Patil,* or cord, is that highly-colored thread which is used to bind together the holy garments of the High Priest.

> He said, 'What pledge shall I give you?' And she said, *'Your seal and your cord,*[31]*and your staff that is in your hand.'* So he gave them to her and went in to her, and she

34

conceived by him. Then she arose
and departed, and *removed her veil
and put on her widow's garments...*
(Ge 38:18-19)

When Judah sent the young goat by
his friend the Adullamite, to receive
the pledge from the woman's hand,
he did not find her. He asked the
men of her place, saying, 'Where is
the temple prostitute who was by
the road at Enaim?' But they said,
'There has been no temple prostitute
here.' So he returned to Judah,
and said, 'I did not find her; and
furthermore, the men of the place
said, "'There has been no temple
prostitute here.'" Then Judah said,
'Let her keep them, otherwise we will
become a laughingstock. After all, I
sent this young goat, but you did not
find her.'

Now it was about three months later
that Judah was informed, *'Your
daughter-in-law Tamar has played
the harlot, and behold, she is also
with child by harlotry.'* Then Judah
said, 'Bring her out and let her be
burned!' It was while she was being
brought out that she sent to her
father-in-law, saying, "I am with
child by the man to whom these
things belong.' And she said, *'Please
examine and see*, whose signet ring
and cords and staff are these?'
Judah recognized them, and said,
'She is more righteous than I...'
(Ge 38:20-26)

**Tamar's question to Judah is exactly what Judah's
question was to Jacob when he brought Joseph's**

blood-stained coat to his father Jacob. Please examine this garment. Is this your son's garment or not?

Without Tamar's righteousness and brave actions, Judah would have had no offspring to perpetuate in the Land, the Covenant, and among the People of Messiah. Tamar asks for Judah's signs of authority, his staff, his seal, and his cord. Two of these emblems are extended to Queen Esther as well. The signet ring is her authority to write in the name of the King, and twice the King extends his scepter, the royal staff of authority and favor.[32] Judah's tribal blessing is to hold the scepter in Israel. Courageously, Tamar does not allow this blessing or Judah's royal lineage to be cut off from Israel.

32. "The scepter is symbolic of rulership. By extending the scepter, the King demonstrates that he is taking her (Esther) under his protection." (Zlotowitz, 2003, p. 84.)

There is another stranger who is of questionable character, Rahab. Although called a prostitute, and although she has no husband, she is a virtuous, heroic, woman:

33. Joshua in Hebrew is Yehoshua. Its shortened form is Yeshua, the name of Messiah. Hebrew names are sometimes shortened in a contraction, such as Elisha (אלישע) is the contracted form of Elishua (אלישוע), dropping the Hebrew letter vav ו and its vowelization. This example of Elisha/Elishua is in Thayer's Lexicon entry to Strong's H477 & H474.

- Aiding and abetting the return of Israel to the *Land* of Israel
- Marrying into the *Covenant of Torah*, she acquires a husband, Joshua[33]
- Becoming part of the *People* of the Covenant
- Producing *offspring* of the Covenant in the Land

Examine the following passages closely for the context clues:

> The men said to her, 'We shall be free from this oath to you which you have made us swear, unless when we come into the land, you tie this *cord of scarlet thread* in the window through which you let us down, and *gather to yourself into the house your father and your mother and*

*your brothers and all your father's
household.* It shall come about that
anyone who goes out of the doors of
your house into the street, his blood
shall be on his own head, and we
shall be free; but anyone who is with
you in the house, his blood shall be
on our head if a hand is laid on him.'
(Jo 2:17-19)

So the *young men* who were spies
went in and brought out Rahab and
her father and her mother and her
brothers and all she had; they also
brought out all her relatives and
placed them outside the camp of
Israel. They burned the city with fire,
and all that was in it. *Only the silver
and gold*, and articles of bronze and
iron, *they put into the treasury of the
house of the LORD.* However, *Rahab
the harlot and her father's household
and all she had, Joshua spared; and
she has lived in the midst of Israel to
this day, for she hid* (covered) *the
messengers* whom Joshua sent to
spy out Jericho. (Jo 6:23-25)

Tamar and Rahab were thought to be prostitutes, but
they turned out to be virtuous women who ensured
the Children of Israel were perpetuated to live in the
Land and Covenant. Like Ruth, they were strangers
and widows welcomed because of their virtuous,
heroic actions. The virtuous woman of Proverbs
Thirty-one is actually a "woman of valor," like a
soldier, *chayil*, a hero in a time of crisis. Prophetically,
the stranger has a place in the covenant.

5

IS SHE YOUR SISTER, MISTER?

What other hidden identities form a pattern? One is the sister, like Dinah. Miriam was the sister of Moses and Aaron. Leah and Rachel were sisters. Moses discovered his wife Tzipporah with her sisters; all were first identified with a well or body of water. Our first example, Dinah, was a sister of the twelve tribes. The matriarchs had a pattern of concealing their spousal relationship with the mask of a sister:

> It came about when he came near to Egypt, that he said to Sarai his wife, 'See now, I know that you are a beautiful woman; and when the Egyptians see you, they will say, "'This is his wife'"; and they will kill me, but they will let you live. Please say that you are my sister so that it may go well with me because of you, and that I may live on account of you.'

> It came about when Abram came into Egypt, the Egyptians saw that the woman was very beautiful. Pharaoh's officials saw her and praised her to Pharaoh; and the woman was taken into Pharaoh's

house. Therefore, he treated Abram
well for her sake; and gave him
sheep and oxen and donkeys and
male and female servants and
female donkeys and camels.

But the LORD struck Pharaoh and his
house with great plagues because
of Sarai, Abram's wife. Then Pharaoh
called Abram and said, 'What is this
you have done to me? Why did you
not tell me that she was your wife?
Why did you say, "'She is my sister,'"
so that I took her for my wife? Now
then, here is your wife, take her and
go.' Pharaoh commanded his men
concerning him; and they escorted
him away, with his wife and all that
belonged to him. (Ge 12:11-20)

So Abram went up from Egypt to
the Negev, he and his wife and all
that belonged to him, and Lot with
him. Now Abram was very rich in
livestock, in silver and in gold.
(Ge 13:1-2)

Now Abraham journeyed from
there toward the land of the Negev,
and settled between Kadesh and
Shur; then he sojourned in Gerar.
Abraham said of Sarah his wife, 'She
is my sister.' So Abimelech king of
Gerar sent and took Sarah. But God
came to Abimelech in a dream of
the night, and said to him, 'Behold,
you are a dead man because of
the woman whom you have taken,
for she is married.' Now Abimelech
had not come near her; and he
said, 'Lord, will You slay a nation,
even though blameless? Did he

not himself say to me, "'She is my sister?'" And she herself said, "'He is my brother.'" In the integrity of my heart and the innocence of my hands I have done this…"
(Ge 20:1-16)

Then Abimelech called Abraham and said to him, 'What have you done to us? And how have I sinned against you, that you have brought on me and on my kingdom a great sin? You have done to me things that ought not to be done.' … Abraham said, 'Because I thought, surely there is no fear of God in this place, and they will kill me because of my wife. Besides, she actually is my sister, the daughter of my father, but not the daughter of my mother, and she became my wife;' and it came about, when God caused me to wander from my father's house, that I said to her, 'This is the kindness which you will show to me: everywhere we go, say of me, "'He is my brother.'"

Abimelech then took sheep and oxen and male and female servants, and gave them to Abraham, and restored his wife Sarah to him. Abimelech said, 'Behold, my land is before you; settle wherever you please.' To Sarah he said, 'Behold, I have given your brother a thousand pieces of silver; behold, it is your vindication before all who are with you, and before all men you are cleared.' (Ge 20:1-16)

So Isaac lived in Gerar. When the

men of the place asked about his wife, he said, 'She is my sister,' for he was afraid to say, 'my wife,' thinking, the men of the place might kill me on account of Rebekah, for she is beautiful. It came about, when he had been there a long time, that Abimelech king of the Philistines looked out through a window, and saw, and behold, Isaac was caressing his wife Rebekah.

Then Abimelech called Isaac and said, 'Behold, certainly she is your wife! How then did you say, "'She is my sister '"? And Isaac said to him, 'Because I said, "'I might die on account of her.'" Abimelech said, 'What is this you have done to us? One of the people might easily have lain with your wife, and you would have brought guilt upon us.' So Abimelech charged all the people, saying, 'He who touches this man or his wife shall surely be put to death.' (Ge 26:6-11)

Now Isaac sowed in that land and reaped in the same year a hundredfold. And the LORD blessed him, and the man became rich, and continued to grow richer until he became very wealthy; for he had possessions of flocks and herds and a great household, so that the Philistines envied him. (Ge 26:12-14)

Notice that in each case above, the sister-wife's reputation and virtue was put in jeopardy because of envy and/or covetousness. Even Jacob relied on two sisters for counsel in leaving his sojourning with Laban to return to the Land, Covenant, and People of Israel. The two sisters point out to Jacob that they have no inheritance in the Land of Laban. They see that he no longer looks at Jacob the way he did. Laban is envious of Jacob's wealth, and he feels as though it should be his. The sisters believe they were sold by Laban, and there is nothing for them or their children. The sisters know that their future health and wealth, the inheritance of their children, depends upon Jacob's return to the Land of Promise with the sheep.

The sisters give counsel: Jacob, return to the Land of Promise with all "these" children and the streaked, striped, and speckled goats and sheep, oxen, donkeys, and nursing camels. Return to the altar of your father Abraham, Jacob, and take the many-colored flocks and herds with you. Redeem the nations from the Land of Laban, and surely El Shaddai will meet us there to help us. We must, however, leave in secret, a three-day head-start. The reader heard these words of the righteous journey to the Promised Land as well:

> Then they said, 'The God of the
> Hebrews has met with us. Please,
> let us go a *three days' journey* into
> the wilderness that we may sacrifice
> (*chag*) to the LORD our God,
> otherwise He will fall upon us with
> pestilence or with the sword.' [34]
> (Ex 5:3)

It wasn't just the Israelites who were delivered from Egypt. A mixed multitude went out of Egypt with Israel along with all their flocks, herds, silver and gold! In every place of potential captivity or adultery, the captor's house was struck or threatened with plague, and the virtuous woman is vindicated and goes free. Strangely, Moses tells Pharaoh that the Israelites will be struck with a plague if they don't go three days' journey to celebrate a feast to the God of the Hebrews. When Pharaoh refuses to let

34. Two of the four Altar Judgments listed in the Prophets

them go, *Egypt* is struck with the plagues instead. The three days' journey is one led of the Holy Spirit, a bride following her husband:

> Go and proclaim in the ears of Jerusalem, saying, 'Thus says the LORD, "'I remember concerning you the devotion of your youth,
> The love of your betrothals,
> Your following after Me in the wilderness, through a land not sown.'" (Je 2:2)

Israel was like Sarah and Rebekah generations before, she is the virtuous woman held illegally by Pharaoh. While Abraham and Isaac feared that they would be overpowered and killed by Pharaoh and Abimelech, the Holy One of Israel had no fear that Pharaoh could overpower Him. If Pharaoh does not release Israel to her betrothal ceremony in the wilderness, then the anger of a jealous Bridegroom will fall on him:

> Put me like a seal over your heart,
> Like a seal on your arm.
> For love is as strong as death,
> Jealousy is as severe as Sheol;
> Its flashes are flashes of fire,
> The very flame of the LORD. (So 8:6)

Ten plagues convinced Pharaoh temporarily, and the destruction at the Reed Sea broke the chains completely.

> Thus they set out from the mount of the LORD *three days' journey*, with the *Ark of the Covenant* of the LORD journeying in front of them for the *three days, to seek out a resting place* for them. (Nu 10:33)

The Land, the Covenant, and the People of peace

seek the Shabbat peace of the Seventh Feast, Sukkot. It began in Egypt with a three-day journey to represent the three days of Passover, Unleavened Bread, and First Fruits of the Barley. An analogy may also be made to include the three pilgrimage "days"[35] of Pesach, Shavuot, and Sukkot. Esther's journey to the King's chamber also took three days. On the third day of the fast during the Days of Unleavened Bread,[36] she dressed in her highly colored royal robes and approached him. Even Esther's story has the element of a jealous husband, the king, who orders the potential violator, Haman (may his name be blotted out), to be hung on the gallows he intended for Mordechai.

The story likely would not have happened if the king knew beforehand who Esther was. Likewise, a Pharaoh arose who didn't know Joseph, and he tried to drown babies in the Nile. A jealous Bridegroom kills him and his warriors in the abyss of the Reed Sea. The woman's captors and potential killers are punished measure-for-measure.

The sisters' advice to return to the home of the patriarchs is applied several times in relation to Biblical prophecy. Three is a number of resurrection. The ill will between Laban and Jacob became more obvious after Laban "put three days' journey between himself and Jacob."[37] The seed which has been hidden, buried, and concealed in the Days of Unleavened Bread can burst forth like the Third Day of Creation to reveal the fruit of the counsel. Counsel is the Third Spirit of Adonai, and it moved on the Third Day of Creation when fruits first appeared in the Earth. Until the Third Day, the potential was there, yet hidden.

Like Esther's hidden identity, these sisters giving counsel to the patriarchs to return the sheep to the Land and Covenant of Israel are cloaking a deeper meaning. They were how the patriarchs were tested as to whether they would protect their sister. Here is

35. Sometimes a "day" in Scripture refers to a period of time, such as "in that day."

36. Zlotowitz, 2003, p. 82

37. Ge 30:36

the not-so-secret secret:

Treasure and guard your sister, the
Holy Spirit[38]

38. Ruach
HaKodesh

6

THE OLD NAG AIN'T WHAT SHE USED TO BE

The Book of Proverbs is much more than wisdom literature. It is full of parables, both of the Holy Spirit and its wicked counterpart, the lamp of the wicked. [39] The practicality of the book conceals its deep, spiritual truths. Among them is the personification of the Holy Spirit as a virtuous wife or faithful woman who enables a man to keep the commandments and live.

> My son, *keep my words and treasure my commandments within you.*
> *Keep my commandments and live,* and my teaching as the apple of your eye. Bind them on your fingers; write them on the tablet of your heart. Say to *wisdom,* 'You are my *sister,'* and call *understanding* your *intimate friend.* (Pr 7:1-4)

Wisdom and Understanding are the first two Spirits of Adonai of the seven that comprise the Holy Spirit, or *Ruach HaKodesh*, in Isaiah.[40] In Proverbs, the sister is the picture and parable of the Ruach HaKodesh that breathes life into the commandments of God.

39. Pr 13:9; 21:4; 24:20

40. Is 11:1-2

Proverbs, which literally does mean "parables,"[41] is filled with understanding concerning good and bad wives. A parable puts human skin on spiritual concepts to help direct human thinking about that concept. A bad wife shames her husband publicly. She leaves him naked, poor, and hungry, like the Laodiceans. A good wife is a blessing given by God. [42]

Here are some examples:

> It is better to live in a corner of a roof than in a house shared with a contentious woman. (Pr 21:9)

> It is better to live in a corner of the roof than in a house shared with a contentious woman. (Pr 25:24)

> A foolish son is destruction to his father, and the contentions of a wife are a constant dripping. House and wealth are an inheritance from fathers, but a prudent wife is from the LORD. (Pr 19:13-14)

While one may smile at the proverbs, the context is long lists of contrasts between righteous and wicked men. The textual and thematic pattern is that such-and-such is the result of a man acting uprightly, such as demonstrating generosity, kindness, self-control, fairness, etc., whereas such-and-such is the result of a man's sins such as lying, laziness, drunkenness, stinginess, etc. The context is that the behavior of a man plays a large part in determining whether his wife is contentious and makes him miserable with her words, or whether she is wise and builds up his spiritual home for himself and their children. Her words can be the dripping faucet or music to his ears.

41. *Mishlei* in Hebrew, from *mashal*, which means to direct something; in this case, to direct thinking.

42. Pr 18:22; 12:4; 5:18-19; 19:14; 31:10-31

Proverbs is teaching that sometimes the woman's voice is a mirror that reflects the husband's behavior or spiritual condition. It is foolish to make a wife raise her voice or nag to be heard if her words are actually spiritual wisdom or common sense that could restore balance in the home. She may be pleading for the husband to set those boundaries of the Torah in his home. If these wise warnings are ignored long enough, they become the nagging, dripping faucet, so get ready to live on the rooftop.

The real danger is when a righteous woman *stops* speaking to correct her home's spiritual apathy. The Ruach contends with human beings to focus their attention on the purposes of Heaven. Humans beings need this constant reminder of their eternal purpose in this mortal life.

When a wife is a blessing of God, she is a gift of the Ruach HaKodesh to her husband; she preserves her family in the lands of Laban, Egypt, Babylon, Assyria, or even among the Philistines inside the Land. She is Wisdom, and she will not allow a man to become comfortable in the land of his sojourning; instead she will point him to the inheritance of Israel: the Land, the Covenant, and the People of inclusion. She will remind him that to grow comfortable with many flocks in the land of Laban is not what it means to be a son of Abraham. He must bring those flocks home and build them shelters of Sukkot.[43]

Sarah, Rebekah, Rachel, Leah, Miriam, Tzipporah, Tamar, Rahab, and other women are pictures of the Ruach HaKodesh[44] working in the lives of the patriarchs and prophets to return them to the Land and Covenant of Israel *along with* the inheritance of the nations represented by silver, gold, male and female servants, sheep, and other clean cattle.

The parables contrast the virtuous women of Israel with the harlot or adulteress, women representing a wicked spirit to lead Israel astray from the covenant:

And I saw among the *naive*, and

43. Ge 33:17

44. Holy Spirit

discerned among the youths a young man lacking sense, passing through *the street near her corner*; and he takes the way to her house, in the twilight, in the evening, in the middle of the night and in the darkness. And behold, a woman comes to meet him, *dressed as a harlot* and cunning of heart. She is boisterous and *rebellious*, her feet do not remain at home; she is *now in the streets, now in the squares, and lurks by every corner.*

So she seizes him and kisses him and with a brazen face she says to him: 'I was due to offer peace offerings; *today I have paid my vows.* Therefore, I have come out to meet you, to seek your presence earnestly, and I have found you. *I have spread my couch with coverings, with colored linens of Egypt. I have sprinkled my bed with myrrh, aloes and cinnamon.* Come, let us drink our fill of love until morning; let us delight ourselves with caresses. For my husband is not at home, he has gone on a long journey; he has taken a bag of money with him, at the full moon he will come home.' (Pr 7:7)

The paying of vows is incorporated into Proverbs Seven. The adulteress pays her vows and calls to the naïve on that day. Paying vows is connected with the *chagim*, the three "foot festivals" of pilgrimage to Jerusalem according to Nahum 1:15:

Behold, on the mountains the feet of him who brings good news, who announces peace! *Celebrate your feasts, O Judah; pay your vows. For never again will the wicked one pass through you; he is cut off completely.*

Making, paying, and annulling vows are an important part of the thread connecting Israel with the nations. Vows connect us to another Torah portion. There are similarities in Proverbs and Prophets that help explain the Torah as well as the Book of Esther. The Holy and evil spirits have many similarities, for Satan comes as an angel of light. Both the Spirit of Wisdom and folly, the woman of valor and the adulterous woman and harlot:

1. call out to the naïve
2. call from the high places and entry points of the city
3. prepare food or a banquet for the naïve
4. mix wine
5. sit at crossroads of the streets (places of decision).
6. arrange coverings for the simple-minded

Sitting at crossroads of the streets is a hint to Rahab the harlot. Her Hebrew name *Rachav* means "a broad place," a place where many people are mixed and directed on the same path. This has a good and bad side. The bad side is mere diversity and mingling with uncleanness. The good side is Sukkot and its diverse kinds of first fruits[45] united in their walk with Messiah.

Mordechai also sits at the King's Gate, which is one of many hints in the Book of Esther to the prophetic work of the Holy Spirit. According to the pattern of the Wise Woman as well as the harlot in Proverbs and the Prophets, Esther also mixes wine and prepares a banquet for the King and Haman to overturn actions and reveal motivations both naïve and wicked.

45. See
*Creation Gospel
Workbook Two*

By arranging coverings for the simple-minded, the women of Proverbs provide another Sukkot hint, which is the central theme of the fall feasts, coverings.[46] Compare the Virtuous Woman in Proverbs 31 to the Scarlet Harlot in Revelation. The identity of a woman, or the Spirit that she represents, is often a question mark in Scripture. Even Esther concealed her identity, but she was Hadassah, the myrtle branch waved toward the four corners of the earth at Sukkot, Tabernacles, to call home Yeshua's sheep.

46. See
*Creation Gospel
Workbook One*

7

YES, YOUR HONOR

The experiences of Jacob's family in the Promised Land while Joseph is exiled to Egypt yield important prophecy links. Yet another thread of a questionable, childless woman at the crossroad provides a strange insertion into the story of Joseph:

> Now after a considerable time Shua's daughter, the wife of Judah, died; and when the time of mourning was ended, Judah went up to his sheepshearers at Timnah, he and his friend Hirah the Adullamite. It was told to Tamar, 'Behold, your father-in-law is going up to Timnah to shear his sheep.' So she removed her widow's garments and covered herself with a veil, and wrapped herself, and sat in the gateway of Enaim, which is on the road to Timnah; for she saw that Shelah had grown up, and she had not been given to him as a wife. When Judah saw her, he thought she was a harlot, for she had covered her face. (Ge 38:12-15)

The area where Tamar would have waited for Judah is north of Jerusalem in the hills around Shechem and Shiloh. Shiloh is in the area of Tapuach and Enaim. The location of Timnah, however, is odd. There are guesses, but there is no Timnah there today, perhaps lost in history. The most probable location where Judah went to shear his sheep is in the general vicinity of Shechem, the area where Joseph was kidnapped and sold. The absence of a Timnah in that area...and the fact that the location is given twice...forces us to look to a Timnah for which we DO know the location.

Timnah is in the extreme south of Israel, intersecting Edom. It was a place of copper mines from which the bronze was made. Bronze denotes fire. The brazen/copper altar was where sacrifices were burned in the wilderness. Tamar was nearly burned until her righteousness was revealed. The road to Timnah is NOT a place of much sheepshearing today. It is abandoned copper mines, red rock, and sand.

Timnah comes from:

> mâna'; a primitive root; to debar
> (negatively or positively) from benefit
> or injury: deny, keep (back), refrain,
> restrain, withhold.

The First Mention of manah is a similar context:

> Then Jacob's anger burned
> against Rachel, and he said,
> 'Am I in the place of God, who
> has withheld [manah H4513] from
> you the fruit of the womb?' (Ge 30:2)

The designation of Timnah may be a way of emphasizing a message. Judah and his sons had withheld children from righteous Tamar. She was thought to be noble, a descendant of Shem, Malkhi-tzedek, the priest of Shalem.

Tamar = palm tree, a symbol of righteousness

There is a Tamar on the road to Timnah. It fits the Biblical description, which suggests a "crossroad." Biblical Tamar is on the ancient Spice Route. To the east is Petra and Moab; the road to the north goes to Judea; the road west goes to Beer Sheba and Egypt; and to the south the road goes to Edom and the Timnah copper mines.

Ezekiel 47:19 and 48:28 mention Tamar as marking the southern border of Israel:

> The south side (*negev*) toward the south (*temanah*) shall extend from Tamar as far as the waters of Meribath-kadesh, to the brook of Egypt and to the Great Sea. This is the south side (*temanah*) toward the south (*negbah*). (Eze 47:19)

Notice the pattern of the words describing Tamar's location in a chiasm:

- Negev
- **Temanah**
- **Temanah**
- Negbah

In a chiasm, the axis, or middle of the mirror, describes the essence of the embedded message. [47] In the case of Tamar, her essence, *temanah*, is "toward Teman," or Timnah. This may be a subtle pointer. Timnah is in the territory of Edom, the Red One, or Esau. Symbolically, the identity of Edom has transformed over the centuries. At first, the Edomites were simply the descendants of Esau, a literal brother to Israel. Later, Edom was thought to have given rise to Rome, and even the Romans have a tradition of Romulus and Remus, twins, and the founding of

47. Go to the Appendix for an exercise that demonstrates how a chiasm works.

55

Rome by Romulus. This is reminiscent of the Jacob/ Esau story. Later, the identity of Edom morphed into the Roman Church and Holy Roman Empire, which was the continuation of the Roman Empire. Without pursuing a long prophecy trail, one may loosely define Edom as an aspect of the nations:

> Who is this who comes from *Edom*,
> With garments of *glowing colors* from Bozrah,
> This One who is majestic in His apparel,
> Marching in the greatness of His strength?
> 'It is I who speak in righteousness, mighty to save.'
> Why is Your apparel *red*,
> And Your garments like the one who treads in the *wine press*?
> 'I have trodden the wine trough alone,
> And *from the peoples* there was no man with Me.
> I also trod them in My anger
> And trampled them in My wrath;
> And their *lifeblood* is sprinkled on My garments,
> And I stained all My raiment.'
> (Is 63:1-3)

Isaiah's prophecy suggests that Messiah will come "from the peoples" when he marches back to Jerusalem. His physical route is described from the area of Edom and Bozrah, which would take him through Tamar slightly west at a crossroad. Messiah's garments are stained red, the color of Edom. The mountains of Edom and Timnah are the purest red. The "spiritual" location of Tamar then, may be a prophecy of Messiah, for the decisions of Judah and Tamar at that crossroad form the axis of the story of Joseph and the eventual family reunion.

Tamar's first two husbands, the sons of the Canaanite woman, were Er and Onan. They were called "evil in the eyes of Hashem." They wasted more than their seed. They wasted a righteous woman's precious time. Likewise, Judah wasted Tamar's time waiting for a son he never intended to give to her in marriage. After much waiting, Tamar reached a crossroad of decision. Where Tamar sat in wait for Judah has been translated differently by Christian and Jewish scholars (Ge 38:14):

> NASB: "So she removed her widow's garments and covered herself with a veil, and wrapped herself, and sat in the gateway of Enaim, which is on the road to Timnah..."

> Artscroll/Rashi: "So she removed her widow's garb from upon her, covered herself with a veil, and wrapped herself; and she sat *at a crossroads* which is on the road toward Timnah..."

The key is at the crossroads.

These subplots describe how the children of Jacob "dwell" in the Land and in exile. *Vah-teshev* describes Tamar's sitting, *yashav*, in the feminine form of the verb. Her story is in the Torah portion *Va-yeishev*, which describes Jacob's dwelling in the Promised Land in the masculine form of the verb. Tamar dwells "at the opening of eyes on the way to Timnah" because she "saw" Judah intended to withhold Shelah and children from her. What happens at Tamar's dwelling will open Judah's eyes. A crossroads is called an "opening of the eyes" because it is the point at which the traveler must open his eyes, to decide which way to go.[48]

When Tamar is found to be pregnant, Judah judges her, sentencing her to death by burning. If she were

48. Rashi to Genesis 38:14

57

a daughter or descendant of Shem, it would make sense, for he was a priest, and burning was the penalty for a licentious daughter of a priest.

Rather than shame his honor Judah, the progenitor of the monarchal dynasty of Israel, Tamar waits until the last moment to produce the three emblems of Mashiach (Messiah): the staff, the signet ring, and the garment cord. The staff is both a shepherd's staff and an object of tribal authority. It is a sign of Mashiach: "And there shall come forth a rod from the stem of Jesse."[49] Judah's garment cord was like a husband covering his wife with his tallit at a Jewish marriage ceremony; it is decorated by highly-colored cords of blue. The signet ring was that which sealed legal agreements. Tamar procured Judah's agreement to marriage. Judah even called her a play-on word, *ha-kedeshah*, "the holy," which can also mean a temple prostitute. When she vanishes without taking payment of a kid from the flock, Judah doesn't seek the "prostitute" because he doesn't want the shame of the matter to become known.

Rather than diminish his honor, Tamar gives Judah a chance to have her killed so that his transgression will not be found out. He can seek the wrong kind of honor among his peers and family. She asks at the last opportunity, "as she was taken out"[50]: "Do you recognize these?" Judah had asked this question of his father Jacob when he deceived him with Joseph's torn, bloody garment, blood taken from a "kid." When Tamar produces the three personal emblems, Judah understands a deeper question. Do you "see" your deception and dishonor to your father? Your decision in this matter will lead to a decision in that matter concerning Joseph. Your decision on the road to Timnah will lead to decisions later on the road to and from Egypt.

49. Is 11:1

50. Ge 38:25

Conceal temporary shame, or be shamed now in order to obtain the honor of human nobility cast in the image of Elohim? Judah chose not to be honored for the person he wasn't...and in that decision, he exercised that nobility that Tamar saw in him.

The gift of Tamar is her exemplary ability to salvage Judah's honor even when he hypocritically sentences her to burning. She gives him the opportunity to choose his type of shame and honor. She sacrifices her own honor to open his eyes honorably. An eye, or *ayin*, in Hebrew is also a spring or well. There is a well at ancient Biblical Tamar on the road to Timnah, but there is another spring nearby, literally named Ein Tamar. Whether this was the actual site of the meeting (not probable), it is definitely a teaching location of *spiritual* meaning.

Sometimes the faithful must be respectful and honor those who are behaving dishonorably. A believer must see something in them that they have not yet seen in themselves. And this is why one must continue interceding and intersecting the lives of those who have turned aside from their most noble created selves. See the image of Elohim in others. This is the work of the Ruach HaKodesh.

8

THE QUEEN MOTHER

The Book of Proverbs offers the contrast between the Tamars and Sarahs of Israel and the adulteresses and harlots. Strangely, the behaviors of the wicked often mimic the covenant behaviors of the righteous. Even the wicked spirit has some acquaintance with the vows and feasts of virtuous Israel. She knows where her husband is and when his appointed time of return is, at the full moon. Her festival times are empty of holiness and full of wickedness.

> Then it will come about that any who
> are left of all the nations that went
> against Jerusalem will go up from
> year to year to worship the King, the
> LORD of hosts, and to celebrate the
> Feast of Tabernacles. (Zec 14:16)

Jerusalem is the center of the festivals of Adonai. This is where Israel and all nations are taught to worship Adonai at the appointed times. To return to the festivals is to return to Jerusalem. To return to the festivals is to regain the strength of the Ruach HaKodesh, submitting to the spiritual commandments, the testimony of Yeshua that is the inheritance of the nations.

Pesach, Shavuot, and Sukkot were times of paying

vows. The harlot tells the naïve that

1. She has paid her vows, which connects her with a feast day and
2. Her husband will not return until the full moon. Sukkot is a full moon, as is Unleavened Bread. She could be prophetically telling the naïve that they can enjoy their love affair until Sukkot.

The theme of vows along with the moedim/chagim, the adulteress woman, the virtuous woman, and Queen Esther needs further study. The 7th feast is the Feast of Sukkot, the Feast of the Nations. Is Queen Esther, Hadassah, really a representative of the nations? If Queen Esther is a picture of Sukkot, the Spirit of Reverence, the 7th Spirit and 7th Feast and Shabbat, then where are the clues of the 7s in the text of the *Megillah*[51] of Esther? It is full of them, just like Revelation. Here is a partial list:

- The King calls for Queen Vashti on the seventh day.
- He sends seven eunuchs with the message.
- The King confers with seven officers for judgment.
- Esther had seven special maids.
- Esther was taken to the palace in the seventh year of the reign.

Queen Esther is the queen of a far-flung Persian empire that encompasses many peoples and nations under King Achashverosh's rule. He is attempting to unify these many peoples, which he tried to accomplish with the feasting that ultimately resulted in Queen Vashti's demise. Vashti's refusal to appear as a queen before the nations of the earth led to the promotion of Queen Esther. With her mysterious background, Esther could be rightly promoted as a Queen of the Nations, her very anonymity making her an inspiration of inclusion for all in the Kingdom. [52]

51. scroll

52. Fohrman, 2011, p. 34

Sarah, the foundational matriarch with a promise to become the mother of many nations, lived 127 years.[53] Queen Esther ruled with King Achashverosh over 127 provinces. Sarah birthed the nations, and Queen Esther united them under one king! This is the gathering of the nations in prophecy, and Queen Esther is fulfilling her role in her generation.

Although Israel has been exiled from the Land, they have not been separated from the Covenant or the People in their exile. Although scattered throughout all the provinces of the Persian Empire for seventy years of exile, they have retained their identity as *am-echad*, a united people. In fact, Haman's complaint to King Achashverosh is that this certain people continue to keep their own laws, not the king's. To fulfill the pattern of the matriarchs who have gone before, Queen Esther will have to reveal her identity with the Land, the Covenant, and the People of Israel. While there are yet years of exile to fulfill, Esther becomes an instrument of salvation to preserve Israel within those nations of the earth.

A slight difference appears in the Book of Esther in relation to the pattern. While Sarah, Rebekah, and Tamar's hidden identities jeopardized their marriage relationship with their husbands, Esther will actually marry a Gentile king, and the doubt of her virtue is subtler in the text. The events in Esther, however, are not to direct our thinking about the direct offspring of Esther as native-born Israelites. A shift occurs, and Queen Esther directs our thinking to a Mother in Israel who will unite nations, tribes, and tongues. In fact, there was so much fear of judgment after Esther and Mordechai's edict that many among those foreign provinces claimed to be Jewish who were not. A seed was planted among the nations that would direct their thinking toward a Land, a Covenant, and a People of Israel.

The Scroll of Esther is full of subtleties. The book is exceptional because the actual Name of God is not

53. Ge 23:1

mentioned. He is like a director working behind the scenes through each of the characters, masked and covered, yet fully engaged in the work of salvation. Even in the Babylonian exile, the work of salvation continues. Had the Jews not been scattered to the 127 provinces, that seed of identity with Israel would not have been planted.

Even the pain of exile can put the faithful in a position to gather the strangers among the nations to Sukkot just as the Israelites did in Egypt. The strangers who could potentially be gathered may even be eunuchs, symbolized by the eunuchs who took care of Queen Esther and gave her favor:

> Thus says the LORD, 'Preserve justice and do righteousness, for *My salvation* is about to come and My righteousness to be revealed. How blessed is the man who does this, and the son of man who takes hold of it; who keeps from profaning the sabbath, and keeps his hand from doing any evil. Let not the foreigner who has joined himself to the LORD say, 'The LORD will surely separate me from His people.' Nor let the eunuch say, 'Behold, I am a dry tree.' For thus says the LORD, 'To the eunuchs who keep My sabbaths, and choose what pleases Me, and hold fast My covenant, to them I will give in My house and within My walls a memorial, and a name better than that of sons and daughters; I will give them an everlasting name which will not be cut off.' Also the foreigners who join themselves to the LORD, to minister to Him, and to love the name of the LORD, to be His servants, *everyone who keeps from profaning the sabbath and holds fast*

My covenant...' (Is 56:1-6)

Isaiah's prophecy of inclusion foretells a miraculous time when those previously excluded from Temple worship are accepted because of their faithfulness to the Torah covenant. A eunuch, like a stranger, had no place of inclusion in Temple worship because of a physical defect through no fault of his own. Neither does a stranger control into which family he is born. Instead of admittance because of physical perfection or pedigree, the eunuch and stranger are brought near because of their faithfulness to the Covenant:

> Even those I will bring to My holy
> mountain and make them joyful
> in My house of prayer. Their burnt
> offerings and their sacrifices will
> be acceptable on My altar; for
> My house will be called a house of
> prayer for all the peoples. The Lord
> GOD, who gathers the dispersed
> of Israel, declares, 'Yet others I will
> gather to them, to those already
> gathered.' All you beasts of the field,
> all you beasts in the forest, come to
> eat. His watchmen are blind, all of
> them know nothing. All of them are
> mute dogs unable to bark, dreamers
> lying down, who love to slumber;
> and the dogs are greedy, they are
> not satisfied. And they are shepherds
> who have no understanding; they
> have all turned to their own way,
> each one to his unjust gain, to the
> last one. 'Come,' they say, 'let us
> get wine, and let us drink heavily of
> strong drink; and tomorrow will be
> like today, only more so.' (Is 56:7-12)

A House of Prayer for All Nations is the goal of The Good Shepherd.   Joseph, a prophecy of Rachel's children and their "companions"[54] hidden among the nations of exile is the one who conceives children outside the Land and unites estranged brothers in his variety of "hidden" roles. He was kidnapped by his brothers while they were in the field with the sheep. Joseph's name alludes to Asiph, the Feast of Sukkot and gathering of righteous first fruits from the nations.

54. Ezek 37:16

9

CHARTER PLAIN

There are so many parallels between Joseph and
the Scroll of Esther, it is easier to list them as a chart.
When placed side-by-side, the story within the story
becomes much plainer.

Joseph	Esther
Joseph was kidnapped and sold to a high-ranking Egyptian officer.	Esther was taken by king's officers to the palace.
Joseph served in house of Potiphar and prison with great favor.	Esther was given favor with the eunuchs in the preparation harem.

Joseph was accused of the attempted seduction of Potiphar's wife.	Haman puts Esther in a compromising position when he pleads for his life on her couch. Esther is not clear in the first invitation whether the banquet was prepared for the King or Haman: "Esther said, 'If it pleases the king, may the king and Haman come this day to the banquet that I have prepared for *him*.'" (Est 5:4) This makes the king think so hard he can't sleep that night, and it leads to the discovery that Mordechai's good deed went unrewarded. Imagine what the king thought when he saw Haman across her couch.
Joseph was imprisoned, and could have been put to death because of Potiphar's *wife's* testimony.	Haman's *wife* advised him to build a gallows for Mordechai.
Joseph was kept in prison.	Esther was guarded in a harem.
Joseph interpreted Pharaoh's troubling dreams and was exalted.	Mordechai is exalted like the king when the king's sleep is shaken.

Joseph changed clothes to appear before Pharaoh.	Esther changed clothes to fit her different situations; Esther and the King both send clothes to Mordechai.
Joseph marries a Gentile, daughter of the Priest of On. *On* is a sound-alike with some similar meanings to the Hebrew *on*, alluding to *Oni* or *Ani*, suffering, the poor. The Passover Unleavened Bread is *ha-lachma anyah*, and Benjamin's first name was Ben-*oni*..	Esther marries the Gentile king of the empire, the known world, whose banquet includes all subject nations, alluding to the feast of Sukkot; the final feast of the moedim. A marriage feast was held, like Sukkot.
Jacob believes Joseph has been torn by wild beasts, a jealous spirit and an altar judgment. [55]	Esther battles a wild beast Haman, which is a jealous spirit and altar judgment.
Described as a beautiful man.	Esther is beautiful.
Joseph's eventual deliverance is a result of two of king's servant's being suspected of subterfuge: one a wine cupbearer, one a baker.	Mordechai saves the king from an assassination attempt by two who plotted against him.
The baker is hanged; cupbearer is delivered.	Haman is hanged, but Esther, who devises specifically a wine banquet, is delivered with her people.

55. The four altar judgments are famine, sword, pestilence, and wild beasts. See *Creation Gospel Workbooks Two and Four* for a more complete treatment of the four altar judgments

The cupbearer's dream was of three tendrils of grapes which he squeezed in to Pharaoh's cup. The baker's dream was of three baskets of baked goods. Each dream represented three days and a symbol of Sukkot: grapes and basket. The cupbearer was restored after three days, and the baker was hanged, just like Haman. Joseph at first put the brothers in prison for three days.	Esther prepared the wine for the king and Haman on the third day, but she revealed her true identity and the plot on the fourth at another wine banquet. The revelation of evil took place during days of Unleavened Bread, chiastic to the season of fall feasts, including Sukkot.[56] Esther had the Jews fast for three days.
Joseph planned a banquet to set up his brothers and expose their evil.	Esther planned a banquet to set up Haman and expose his evil.
Joseph wept bitterly when he saw Benjamin, who been subject to the brothers' unwitting death decree spoken by Judah.	Esther, a Benjamite, wept before the king when he could not reverse the death decree against Judah.
Joseph's sale into slavery was the result of his brothers' envy and jealousy.	The genocide decree against the Jews was because of Haman's jealousy of Mordechai.

56. See *Creation Gospel Workbook One* for examples and a complete explanation of chiasms, or mirror-structures, or complete the chiastic menorah cut-out in the Appendix.

When Jacob finds out he must send Benjamin to Egypt, he says, "If I am bereaved, I am bereaved."[57]	When Esther finds out that she must go to the king unbidden, she says, "If I am lost, I am lost."
Joseph is elevated to second-in-command to Pharaoh because of the failure of the fortunetellers and advisors.	Esther is made second in the nation because of Vashti's failure to appear, which displeased the king.
Pharaoh's dream is about famine, an altar judgment.	The king's sleep is "shaken" so that he be reminded of the murder plot against him, the altar judgment of sword.
Joseph hides his true identity from his brothers. Devises a plan for their unification and salvation.	Esther hides her true identity in the Persian palace. Devises a plan for the protection of the "nation" within empire and their salvation.
Joseph is made second in command to Pharaoh: horses, robes, jewelry, and signet ring to administrate.	Esther is second to the king along with Mordechai: horse, robes, jewelry/crown, and signet ring to administrate.
Joseph is given a different name when he's Pharaoh's viceroy; his real name hints to Sukkot.	Esther is given a different name when she lives in the palace; her real name hints to Sukkot.

57. The verb Jacob uses twice – *shakolti* – literally means to lose a child. His phrase begins with the Hebrew word *ka'asher* and is followed by a doubled verb, *shakolti, shakolti*, each phrased in first person, past tense. The only other time in the entire Bible *ka'asher* appears along with a similarly conjugated doubled verb is when Esther says *ka'asher avadeti, avadeti*, "*If I am lost, I am lost*." (Fohrman, 2011, p. 133).

Joseph gives Judah the opportunity to become a deliverer and substitute sacrifice for Benjamin.	As a Benjamite, Esther has the opportunity to lay down her life for "the Jews," Judah and/or become Judah's deliverer.
Joseph prepares a banquet for his brothers as part of his plan. He arranges them by order of seniority/authority after he has accused them of being spies.	Esther prepares a banquet for the king and Haman as part of her plan. The grammar of her first request puts the guest of honor in question. [58] She accuses Haman of abusing the King's authority and insubordination by putting the Queen of his Empire in danger.
Ten of his brothers participated in the plan to sell Joseph.	The king has ten of Haman's sons hanged on the tree, presumably who were complicit in the plot. Haman was an Amalekite, a son of Eliphaz, son of Esau, a brother to Jacob.
Joseph speaks another language in front of his brothers; his decree against Benjamin is in the Egyptian language.	Esther speaks the language of the Persian king, and the decree is made in the language of the king, yet translated to every language.

58. The ambiguous request is worded, "Let the King and Haman come to a banquet I have prepared for HIM." The objective pronoun does not match the subject. It is unclear which man is the guest of honor.

Joseph improves the position of the Israelites and makes them secure in the famine, one of the four altar judgments.	Esther and Mordechai improve the position of the Jews in the kingdom and make them more secure from the threat of sword, one of the four altar judgments.
Joseph's original disagreement with his brothers was over authority, but he eventually uses his authority for good and for life.	Haman uses authority issues to secure an evil decree, but Esther uses the king's authority for good and for life.
Joseph is remembered for a good deed done two years before while he is in prison.	Mordechai is remembered for a good deed done possibly years before.
Joseph works alone in his plan but has Pharaoh's help and authority to unite and save Israel's children.	Esther is preserved by a male cousin's counsel and saved by her husband the king. She is enabled by both men to rule with them so that she can unite Judah spiritually within the empire and save them.

Judah pleads for Benjamin to Joseph, "How could I bear to see the terrible fate that befalls my father?" The message is that he does not want to be spared if his brother Benjamin is not.	Esther pleads for Judah when she pleads for the king to reverse the decree, "How could I bear to see the terrible fate that befalls my people?" With the exception of a single syllable, Esther's words are a direct quote from Judah's. Even that different symbol is a sound-alike. Judah says, "my father," *avi*. Esther says, "my people," *ami*.
In the midst of the story of Joseph there is a smaller one concerning Judah and Tamar. It concerns the emblems of his authority: the garment, the ring, and the staff that verify Tamar's righteousness in ensuring the sons and seed of Judah continue. She bears him twins and becomes part of his house.	Twice the king extends the scepter (king's staff) to Esther, symbolically stating she is under his protection. He also gives her the house of her enemy and his signet ring to write with his authority so that the sons and seed of Judah continue.
Joseph is sold for silver by his brothers, who are jealous.	The Jews are sold for silver by Haman, who is jealous.

Joseph was orphaned of his mother Rachel only.	Esther was doubly orphaned of both father and mother. Orphans receive special attention at Sukkot.
The Threes: Joseph is thirty years old when he stands before Pharaoh. Thirty = Hebrew letter *lamed*, which denotes teaching and learning	Vashti's disobedience was in 3rd year of the reign. The *pur* (lot) was cast in the month of Nissan, the month of Passover, which encapsulates feasts 1-3.
The Sevens: For seven years Joseph prepares for famine, and for seven years he manages the trouble and wrath of famine. Pharoah's dream involved cattle and grains, both emblems of Sukkot offerings, which may come from flocks, herds, winevat, or threshing floor. Sukkot is the 7th Feast.	Esther is taken to the palace in the 7th year of the reign, and the King gives a banquet and gifts for Esther's Banquet, like Sukkot. Esther is in the palace for seven years of good before she must manage the period of trouble. She is in place because Vashti failed to appear on the 7th day summons from the king, a hint to Sukkot. Vashti's failure to appear was feared to cause trouble and wrath among all the provinces of the empire. Sukkot is a time of gathering nations to the feast.

Joseph works alone in his secret plan to unite Israel's children, but his servants are in on it.	Esther coordinates the secret plan of salvation, and her servants fast with her.
Young Joseph dreams that his brothers will bow to him, but they won't.	Haman wants Mordechai to bow to him, but he won't.

10

THE GAMBLER

The threat of adultery appears repeatedly in the story of redemption. Sarah and Rivkah were put at risk with Pharaoh and Abimelech. By legal custom, Tamar was to have married Judah's youngest son, but Judah had delayed the marriage, so it was thought that Tamar had committed adultery when she began to show her pregnancy. Rahab was thought to be a harlot. However, each of these women proved themselves righteous, courageous, and faithful in affirming the promise of a Land, a Covenant, and a People in Israel.

Although subtler, the question of fidelity is also present in the Scroll of Esther. Esther has requested that the Jews fast and pray for three days. On the third day, associated with resurrection, she approaches the King. Perhaps she knew when she resigned herself, "If I perish, I perish," that although the risk required her voluntary surrender to that possible death, it could also become a resurrection day in a number of ways. On this third day, Queen Esther requests that the King and Haman attend a wine banquet.

The wine banquets hold two mysteries. First, wine is associated with the Feast of Sukkot, which is a time to bring the first fruits from the wine vat. Esther is positioning herself to negotiate salvation not simply for the Jews, but prophetically for the first fruits from among the nations where the Jews have been scattered. In the winepress of the King's wrath, Esther becomes a waving lulav of hadassah branches at Sukkot, waving for the four corners of the Earth where Israel is scattered.

The second mystery is found in the Hebrew grammar of Esther's invitation. In Esther 5:4, she requests, "If it please the King, let the King and Haman come today to the banquet that I have prepared for him." There is the problem. The subject is plural, "the King and Haman," yet the pronoun is singular, "him." She should have said, "a banquet I have prepared for them." This plants a seed of doubt in the King's mind. Is she preparing the banquet for him or Haman?[59]

The King and Haman attend the third-day wine banquet, but Esther still conceals her motive for inviting them...or is it him? Instead of giving a direct answer, Esther requests that they attend another wine banquet the following day, the fourth day. In Revelation, the message to the fourth assembly, Thyatira, marks the transition with the fourth day from "tribulation" to "great tribulation." The King knows Esther is troubled, nevertheless he is even more troubled by nightfall. He can't sleep!

What is he thinking about? Perhaps the relationship between his Queen and his second-in-command, Haman. Why would a woman kept in seclusion with her maids and eunuchs request only Haman's presence along with the King's? How did she know Haman? The King had been the subject of assassination plots before, so what was Haman up to? Not coincidentally, this tribulation of mind keeps the King awake that fourth night, which had already begun at sundown that evening.[60] The text reads more literally than usually is translated in English. It would be better translated as, "The sleep of the King was shaken." He calls for the record books to be

59. Fohrman, 2011, p. 44

60. Jews reckon days from sundown to sundown, or evening to evening, the pattern of Genesis One.

read.

At this point, the King hears about Mordechai's intervention on his behalf when two of his high officers plotted to kill him. At last, a loyal subject, this Jew Mordechai. And wasn't Esther his Queen the one who'd actually informed him of the plot? No wonder the King was troubled. At this opportune moment, Haman enters to request permission to hang Mordechai in advance of the decreed destruction upon the Jews. Speak of the devil!

The King tests Haman with a question, but Haman's pride prevents him from grasping the questions hidden within the question, which might be, "Haman, what are you up to? Are you trying to steal my kingdom and my queen? Second-in-command and my ring aren't enough for you?" The King asks Haman what should be done with a man the King desires to honor. Haman gives the worst possible answer, at least in terms of his personal safety. He suggests adorning the man with things the King has worn or used: a crown, a robe, and a horse.

From the King's troubled perspective, this is virtual confirmation of his suspicions. Haman wants his throne. King Achashverosh orders Haman to do those very things for Mordechai, whom Haman has come to request permission to kill. In fact, Haman had constructed an *etz* on the third day on which to hang Mordechai. The same Hebrew word for tree, *etz*, is used for "gallows." The resurrection Spirit of Etzah, the Third Spirit of Adonai, is pushing something hidden to the surface, and the fourth day has indeed become a turning point for the king, Esther, Haman, Mordechai, the Jews, and the 127 provinces.

At the second wine banquet, the King persists in asking Queen Esther what her hidden problem is. To his horror, he finds out that Haman indeed wants to take what is his, his beloved Queen of all the provinces, the unifying symbol of his kingdom. It is not as he suspects, though, that Haman wants to kill him and possess his Queen; instead, Haman desires to kill the Queen. In a rage, the King walks into the garden, and Haman again does the worst possible thing he could do: he flings himself at Esther on her cushion.[61] When the King returns, he finds Haman in this very compromising position. Had Esther not already revealed Haman's intent to kill her, the King may have come to a different conclusion about their relationship.

The wrath of the King is executed upon Haman and his family, and King Achashverosh gives Esther and Mordechai his signet ring and full authority to write whatever decree they can that will annul the wrath already decreed. They could not reverse his previous decree, but they could write something that would definitely make the wicked among the provinces think twice before they attacked the Jews. To make something of no effect is to make it null, but it does not mean that the original decree or vow did not exist. Its strength has simply been neutralized. With Esther and Mordechai writing with the King's authority, the People of the Covenant are preserved among the provinces to one day return to their Land.

Some conclusions may be appropriate here. The name of Esther's fast and feast is Purim. Most assume, as the text hints, that the *purim*, or lots, cast by Haman against the Jews are what characterize this holiday. Sound-alike words can offer additional hints to Biblical themes and its internal commentaries. The fall feasts' central theme is coverings, which is derived from the middle feast in the fall, Yom HaKippurim. *Creation Gospel Workbook Two* offers a more complete explanation about the hints to coverings associated with the clouds of the Feast of Trumpets and the winged birds with feathers on the Fifth Day of Creation, but Sukkot is an obvious covered shelter of leafy branches.

61. This links the question mark of fidelity with the adulterous woman in Proverbs who has spread coverings upon her couch.

What about Yom HaKippurim, the Day of Coverings, itself? The *kaphar* of *kippur* means a covering, atonement. On Yom HaKippurim,[62] the High Priest can see the covering cherubim in the Holy of Holies when he enters in a cloud of incense, and he makes a covering of blood on the Mercy Seat of the Ark of the Covenant. On the seven-branched menorah, Yom HaKippurim is chiastic[63] to the Feast of Unleavened Bread.[64] During the Days of Unleavened Bread beginning with actual Sabbath day of Unleavened Bread, Israel fasts from all forms of leaven, but on Yom HaKippurim, Israel fasts both food and water for a day. The days of fasting that Esther proclaims for the Jews is during the days of Unleavened Bread.

Ki in Hebrew means "like, similar to." *Pur* is a lot, an object of chance that determines fate. The suffix *im* designates plural. On Yom HaKippurim, the High Priest drew lots, or *purim*, to designate the fate of the two goats, one *L'Adonai*, and one *L'Azazel*. The goat L'Adonai is slaughtered and its blood sprinkled on the Mercy Seat of the Covenant. L'Azazel is taken to the wilderness with all the sins of the nation and pushed over a precipice. In this sense, Yom HaKippurim is "A Day like Purim." One figurative goat is hanged, while the blood of the other is admitted into the Throne Room, the Holy of Holies, and it covers all Israel in safety. Yeshua becomes the "second-in-command" by virtue of his sacrifice.

There are other parallels between Purim and Yom HaKippurim. On Yom HaKippurim, the High Priest must make atonement first for himself; that is, he must cover himself. Afterward he makes atonement for the people. Two specific atonements are required that day. Esther also makes two trips to the "Holy of Holies," the King's inner chamber of his home where one enters only by invitation. Only the King's mercy would spare any uninvited intruder.

This is the same principle applied to the Holy of

62. The literal name of the day is Yom HaKippurim, the Day of Coverings or Atonements

63. See the Appendix

64. See *Creation Gospel Workbook One*

Holies in the Temple. Only the High Priest is invited at a specific time; any other intruder faces death. Interestingly, though, the blood is applied to the Mercy Seat of the Ark of the Covenant.[65] The very name of the Covenant is Mercy, and this is exactly what Esther receives. To merit this mercy, however, Esther must shed her blood, at least figuratively. She must first acknowledge that she deserves to lose her life for approaching, which is the example of the Yom HaKippurim goat that dies "before the Lord."

The first trip to the inner chamber results in Esther's request for the King to save her life personally, just as the High Priest has to make personal atonement. The second trip is to petition for his help in saving the Jews against his earlier decree, which could not be rescinded. It is on the second trip to the inner chamber to touch his scepter that Esther receives the signet ring and the means to annul the evil decree against her nation among the 127 provinces.

65. The "Covenant" is the Torah, the Book of the Covenant ratified between Adonai and Israel at Sinai. A copy of the Torah was put into the Ark of the Covenant as a testimony. This Ark was also called a Mercy Seat, or throne of mercy. The primary description of the Torah Covenant is mercy.

The role of the sacrificed goat may also be pictured by Mordechai's actions. Mordechai was elevated to second in the Kingdom, for he risked his life by refusing to bow to Haman. As a result, he was covered in the King's robes in honor and given the royal horse and crown. In a sense, Mordechai also sacrificed his own adopted daughter Hadassah by insisting that she go to the King unbidden. Scripture appears to present a virtual sacrifice as equivalent to an actual physical death of an animal. Merely the acceptance of one's death for the sake of the Land, Covenant, or People may substitute for the actual death, which may or may not follow. Peter's acceptance of his method of death and the reason for it supports the other examples of the patriarchs, matriarchs, heroes, and heroines of Scripture.

Queen Esther's sacrificial role as a co-heir, "up to half the Kingdom," protected her far-flung people Israel among the nations. Esther knew that going before the King unbidden would be a walk through the valley of the shadow of death, but like the goat L'Adonai, she says, "If I perish, I perish," and she puts on the royal coverings to approach the inner chamber of the King's house. The Ten Awesome Days of repentance between The Feast of Trumpets and the judgment of Yom HaKippurim have a parallel with Haman's ten sons hung with him in judgment. Even the problem with rescinding the King's decree is related to the principles of Yom HaKippurim, which brings atonement for the nation. The decree was "a public law known by the people of the King's provinces – so transgression would be a public offense like the sin of Vashti."[66]

The changing of garments at Yom HaKippurim demonstrates some connections to Esther. In her first visit to the bedchamber of the King, Esther wears very simple garments upon the Chief Eunuch's advice. This wins her personal favor. The High Priest also removed his official ornamented garments when he visited the Holy of Holies on Yom Kippur. When she goes to invite the King to a banquet, Esther changes to royal robes.

This second trip to the inner chamber seems the reverse practice of the High Priest, but a clue is given in the Book of Hebrews, which explains an additional priestly pattern, the pattern of the royal priesthood of Melchi-tzedek, which Yeshua fills. This makes sense. Esther dresses in the simple fashion of the Levitical priesthood's entrance to the Holy of Holies on her first visit to the King, but her successive trip merits the garments of a royal priesthood. Types and shadows are concealed throughout the Scroll of Esther.

One thing we know. King Achashverosh, whose authority was challenged and insulted by a queen who refused to take her place at his side before the nations, selected a virtuous and courageous queen who would. Queen Esther became every man and woman's Queen, for her anonymity made her perfect to represent every people, no matter the social class

66. Zlotowitz, 2003, p. 78

or humble beginning. Vashti's banishment was to ensure "every man should rule his own home and speak the language of his own people."

The King recognized the diversity of Sukkot fruits over which he ruled, and he needed a woman who would nurture them and give each of them rest in their own languages, a provision symbolized by the Holy Spirit on Shavuot (Acts Two). Judaism recognizes that the Torah was offered to the 70 nations at Mount Sinai on Shavuot, each in their own tongue. Shavuot is a preparation for the diversity of gifts at Sukkot. Queen Esther is a woman who embodies the Ruach HaKodesh according to the pattern of the matriarchs. The heart of her husband safely trusts in her to gather the nations. Queen Esther perfectly fulfills her husband's need to draw together his Kingdom in unity.

11

A VOW WITH A WOW

Part of the Torah portion Mattot includes Numbers 30, which is *Nedarim*, "vows." Typically, vows were paid at the three pilgrimage feasts, but what about their origin? In the earlier part of this study, it was explained that sometimes in Scripture a male is given an obligation, but later a woman fulfills it. This example is in the Scroll of Esther. *Nedar*, or vow, in Hebrew, is spelled *nun-dalet-reish*.

Nun = Fish; productiveness, offspring, like fish, is symbolic of men [67] נ

Dalet = Door, 4, symbolic of authority ד

Reish = Head, also symbolic of authority and the ruach [68] ר

A vow is a method by which the man or woman who takes the vow signifies that he or she desires to widen the door of Adonai's authority in his or her life. By dedicating money, objects, etc., the one who takes a vow enlarges the capacity to operate in Kingdom authority by personal sacrifice. It enables the spirit to control the strong desires of the soul. Both men and women may take the Nazirite vow.

67. "I will make you fishers of men..." (Mt 4:19)

68. spirit

85

In Esther, the King has unwittingly allowed Haman to write a decree. A decree can qualify as a type of vow because its motivation is to widen and establish the authority of the king. Haman has accused the Jews among the 127 provinces of defying the king's laws by keeping their own. The decree will re-establish publically the king's authority over his people, just as a vow is paid publically to publish its intent.

There is a part in the Yom HaKippurim service called *Kol Nidrei*, which mean "All Vows." In this part of the service, individuals pray to be released by Adonai from any ill-advised vows they may have taken in the preceding year. This is not an attempt to circumvent the Torah instructions concerning vows, but acknowledges that anyone can make impulsive, short-sighted promises and resolutions. It is a repentant request for mercy, for the time when the High Priest goes before the Mercy Seat is a favorable time to make such a petition.

Here are a few concepts to look for in the vows of Numbers Thirty:

1. A *na'arah*, a young woman of marriageable age.
2. Relationship between the na'arah and her spouse in his house
3. The na'arah in her father's house
4. Silence as affirmation
5. A specific time

The hook between Esther and nedarim, according to Rabbi Fohrman,[69] is the Hebrew word *lehacharish*, which means silence. Mordechai uses the word in succession: *"Im hacharesh tacharishi..."* When words are repeated, it emphasizes a point.

69. p. 108 *L'hacharish* appears as a doubled verb in only one

other place in the entire *Tanakh*. The only other place is in Numbers, Torah portion Mattot, the discussion of nedarim, or "annulment of vows." This passage in the Torah instructs fathers and husbands how to annul a daughter's or young wife's vow if it would bring her undue hardship. He must look out for her best interests, yet allow her to manage her spiritual walk.

There is one important rule, though. If he wants to annul the vow, he must do so *as soon as he hears about it*. He doesn't have days to wait before he objects to it. If he remains silent, then by virtue of his silence, *l'hacharish*, he upholds the vow. This is how a husband or a father deals with a young woman's vows when she is *in his house*, or under his authority. If he remains silent, he cannot later change his mind or speak up. Silence means yes. If he tries to annul it later, *he* must bear the sin.

> No means No.
> Yes means Yes.
> Silence means Yes.
>
> Her husband can **affirm** the vow or her husband can **annul** it. (Nu 30:13)

L'hacharish comes from *charash*, a three-letter root. As a noun, it means a deaf person. Rabbi Fohrman[70] writes that the verb form would seem to mean "to make one's self deaf;" in other words, to choose it. I'm sure there are no husbands who have ever acted as though they didn't hear their wives. Unfortunately, no response always means, "Yes, I agree!"

It's easy to see that Esther has been put in the situation of needing to annul the King's rash decree. However, she is his wife, not his husband or father. Does the Torah extend this obligation to her? Mordechai seems to think so. He says, "If you remain silent *at this time*, salvation will come to the Jews from

70. p. 112

87

somewhere else, but you and your father's house will be destroyed."

Where would he get this idea? The passage in the Torah states,

> Ishah **yekimenah**, v'ishah **yepheirenah**.
> Her husband can **affirm** it; her husband can **annul** it.

Here is the beauty of Hebrew. The Torah did not originally have vowel points, therefore vocalization can change the meaning of a word. In this case, "*ishah*," her husband (ish + ah), can also be translated as "a woman." In this play-on word passage, the text would read,

> A woman. A woman can affirm; a woman can annul.

Mordechai appears to have read a secondary, prophetic double meaning in the Torah passage. It would read that

a. a woman's husband could annul or affirm a vow, *or*

b. a woman could annul or affirm a vow.

All Mordechai had to do was to remove a dot from the *heh* at the end of the word, which was not even in the original text. Mordechai tells Esther that she must attempt to annul her spouse's rash decree, for it was not only unwise in doing damage to his own kingdom, it would damage Esther personally. There was destruction built in the decree to her personally, but according to the passage in Numbers, there would also be a Torah judgment on Esther and her father's house. Mordechai surely understands that the obligation is not Esther's, yet he warns her as though it is.

Mordechai warns Esther that she must give an immediate response in order not to affirm the decree. Esther seems to understand Mordechai's explanation, for she relinquishes her life for her people at that moment. She immediately puts a plan in place to register her objection to her husband.

As a review, *ki* in Hebrew means "like, similar to." *Pur* is a lot, an object of chance that determines fate. On Yom Kippur, the High Priest drew lots, or purim, to designate the fate of the two goats, one *L'Adonai*, and one *L'Azazel*. In this sense, Yom Kippur is "A Day like Purim." One figurative goat is hanged, while the blood of the other is admitted into the Throne Room, the Holy of Holies, and it covers all Israel in safety.

There are two important Hebrew words in Nedarim, "affirm" and "annul." The Hebrew word for annul is *pur*. Affirm is *kayam*. Seven times in Chapter Nine of Esther a form of the word pur, or annul, occurs. There are seven occurrences of the root word *kayam* for affirm in the same chapter. This adds up to 14, the number of Messiah's generations. Seven is Shabbat, Sukkot, the Kingdom. Doubled, it is Messiah's generations, 14. The 7th and last occurrence of both *kayam* and *pur* in Chapter Nine appear in the same verse: "And the decree of Esther *affirmed* these words of *Purim*." One of the themes of Yom Kippur is brotherly, sacrificial love,[71] and Queen Esther perfectly typifies the Day Like Purim. Like her future Messiah, she laid down her life for her friends.

71. See *Creation Gospel Workbook One*

89

12

COVER GIRL

Can you now answer these questions, or would you answer them now differently than you would have answered them the first time?

- Who is Esther?
- Who are the matriarchs and heroines of Scripture? What is the pattern of their thinking and actions?
- Does Esther fit this pattern?
- What is their ultimate goal in concealing identities?
- Who will benefit?

In your answers, you've likely found these unifying themes among the Torah, the Prophets, the New Covenant, and the Scroll of Esther:

- The matriarchs of Israel have a hidden identity that leads to salvation, deliverance, and the return of Israel to the Land, the Torah Covenant, and the People of Israel.
- The original plan provided for the inclusion of both native-born sheep and the Gentile flock gathered from the nations for Sukkot.
- There are similarities between a virtuous woman and a harlot, and their questionable

identity ties them together in prophecy.
- There is a repetition of Joseph's life in Esther.
- There is role reversal, or more accurately, role SHARING of responsibility, which eventually leads to New Covenant *HaBrit HaChadashah* lessons of co-heirs. King Achachverosh prophesied it when he offered Queen Esther up to half the kingdom.
- A prophecy from the Torah will likely be lived in some way by every generation, from the tribulation of Passover to the reward of Sukkot

Queen Esther carried the scarlet thread of redemption in Israel in her generation. The women who went before her in faith risked everything for the sake of the Promise. So did Queen Esther. Recognition of his authority was very important to King Achashverosh, so the reader should not consider lightly that he gave Queen Esther full authority to speak for him to the 127 provinces. He must have had tremendous trust in her to do that without causing confusion and chaos, for he had been warned that Vashti could cause "much contempt and wrath" throughout his kingdom. However, this is what is said of the Virtuous Woman in Proverbs 31: "The heart of her husband does safely trust in her."

Esther's saga is continued in the Book of Nehemiah. Even a quick assessment of the narrative demonstrates a repetition of the themes in Esther, the Torah, and the Prophets. Nehemiah is King Artaxerxes' [72] *cupbearer.* He tasted the King's *wine* to ensure it was not poisoned,[73] and he requested to return to build up the walls of Jerusalem and to aid the *poor* in the wasted province of Judah. Nehemiah laments in 1:3-4: "They said to me, 'The remnant there in the province who survived the *captivity* are in *great distress* and reproach, and the wall of Jerusalem is broken down and its gates are burned with fire.' When I heard these words, I sat

72. Xerxes is assumed to be Esther's husband Achashverosh (Sarshar, 2002, p. 3)

73. Sarshar, 2002, p. 7

down and *wept and mourned* for days; and I was *fasting and praying* before the God of heaven."

Again, the Scriptures take the reader from Passover to Sukkot thematically. Are there any "sisters" who stand out in the narrative? Of all those fathers and sons who helped to rebuild those broken walls of Jerusalem, one family stands out:

> Next to him Shallum the son of Hallohesh, the official of half the district of Jerusalem, made repairs, he and his daughters. (Ne 3:12)

The Gospel of Messiah Yeshua is equal parts tribulation and triumph. Esther was prepared for the King with six months of myrrh, a burial spice sharing the same root as *maror*, the bitter herbs eaten during Passover. She was also prepared with six months of "cosmetics," the beautifying ministrations to prepare a potential Queen of many nations. Shavuot stands between Passover and Sukkot to proclaim the authority of the King. He delivers the daughters and sisters from tribulation and promotes them to royalty.

The daughters and our female servants were released on the fourth feast of Israel, Shavuot, in Acts Two[74] to proclaim the authority, redemption, and salvation of Messiah Yeshua. The Spirit-filled sisters are unmasked, given full authority to speak in the Name of the King of Kings. They are sealed in the Torah Covenant, commissioned to go to the 127 provinces, the 70 nations of the earth, and the four corners of the earth to carry the scarlet thread of Israel among the nations.

Their good news is that through the blood of Messiah Yeshua, even those not Israel by natural birth have been drawn near. They are drawing near to the Land, the Covenant, and the People of Israel by a new birth in Messiah Yeshua.[75] Esther was an orphan, but she was also an adopted daughter. The

74. Refer to text of Acts 2 in the Appendix

75. Ephesians 2

Spirit of adoption has been poured out on our sons AND our daughters. May all Israel receive their sisters and daughters with the joy of Sukkot.

REFERENCES

Alewine, H. (2006). *The Creation Gospel: Workbook One: Seven Days of Creation, Seven Spirits of God, Seven Feasts, Seven Churches of Revelation.* London, KY: The Creation Gospel.

_____ (2012). *The Creation Gospel: Workbook Four, The Scarlet Harlot and the Crimson Thread.* London, KY: The Creation Gospel.

Fohrman, D. (2011). *The Queen You Thought You Knew: Unmasking Esther's Hidden Story.* USA: HFBS Publishing.

Sarshar, H., Editor. (2002). *Esther's Children: A Portrait of Iranian Jews.* Beverly Hills, CA: Center for Iranian Jewish Oral History, Graduate Society Foundation.

Zlotowitz, M., Trans. (2003). *The Megillah: The Book of Esther.* New York: Mesorah Publications.

Scherman, N. & Zlotowitz, M., Eds. (1997). *The Torah: With Rashi's commentary translated, annotated, and elucidated.* Sapirstein Ed. New York: Mesorah Publications, Ltd.

APPENDIX A

Chiastic Cut-out

Instructions:

1. Label each branch of the menorah in this order: Passover, Unleavened Bread, Firstfruits of Barley, Weeks, Trumpets, Atonements, Tabernacles. You can go left to right or right to left.

2. Cut out the menorah and fold it on its axis (Weeks). The feasts that touch or become one are mirrors of one another.

STUDY QUESTIONS

1. What is Queen Esther's Hebrew name? What does it mean? Of which Israelite festival is it a key part?

2. What is Joseph's Hebrew name? What does it mean? Of which Israelite festival is it a key part?

3. What is the Bible saying when it repeatedly quotes from an earlier narrative?

4. What do Sarah, Rebekah, Leah, and Rachel have in common, either literally or figuratively?

5. Who personifies the Holy Spirit in the Book of Proverbs?

6. What is the "cloud" or question hanging over the heads of many righteous women in Scripture?

7. Explain how the Day of Atonements, Yom HaKippurim, is "a day like Purim."

8. Which two tribes of Israel are highlighted in the Scroll of Esther?

9. Give an example of how a commandment directed at males is obeyed by a female.

10. What is similar about the prophetic work of Queen Esther and Joseph?

STUDY EXERCISE

Study the following chapter from the Book of Acts. How many themes, symbols, and connections can you find to Esther's scroll and the story of Joseph?

Acts 2 Shavuot

1 When the day of Pentecost had come, they were all together in one place. 2 And suddenly there came from heaven a noise like a violent rushing wind, and it filled the whole house where they were sitting. 3 And there appeared to them tongues as of fire distributing themselves, and they rested on each one of them. 4 And they were all filled with the Holy Spirit and began to speak with other tongues, as the Spirit was giving them utterance. 5 Now there were Jews living in Jerusalem, devout men from every nation under heaven. 6 And when this sound occurred, the crowd came together, and were bewildered because each one of them was hearing them speak in his own language. 7 They were amazed and astonished, saying, "Why, are not all these who are speaking Galileans? 8 And how is it that we each hear them in our own language to which we were born? 9 Parthians and Medes and Elamites, and residents of Mesopotamia, Judea and Cappadocia, Pontus and Asia, 10 Phrygia and Pamphylia, Egypt and the districts of Libya around Cyrene, and visitors from Rome, both Jews and proselytes, 11 Cretans and Arabs -we hear them in our own tongues speaking of the mighty deeds of God." 12 And they all continued in amazement and great perplexity, saying to one another, "What does this mean?" 13 But others were mocking and saying, "They are full of sweet wine."

Peter's Sermon

14 But Peter, taking his stand with the eleven, raised his voice and declared to them: "Men of Judea and all you who live in Jerusalem, let this be known to you and give heed to my words. 15 For these men are not drunk, as you suppose, for it is only the third hour of the day ; 16 but this is what was spoken of through the prophet Joel : 17 'AND IT SHALL BE IN THE LAST DAYS,' God says, 'THAT I WILL POUR FORTH OF MY SPIRIT ON ALL MANKIND ; AND YOUR SONS AND YOUR DAUGHTERS SHALL PROPHESY, AND YOUR YOUNG MEN SHALL SEE VISIONS, AND YOUR OLD MEN SHALL DREAM DREAMS ; 18 EVEN ON MY BONDSLAVES, BOTH MEN AND WOMEN, I WILL IN THOSE DAYS POUR FORTH OF MY SPIRIT And they shall prophesy. 19 'AND I WILL GRANT WONDERS IN THE SKY ABOVE AND SIGNS ON THE EARTH BELOW, BLOOD, AND FIRE, AND VAPOR OF SMOKE. 20 'THE SUN WILL BE TURNED INTO DARKNESS AND THE MOON INTO BLOOD, BEFORE THE GREAT AND GLORIOUS DAY OF THE LORD SHALL COME. 21 'AND IT SHALL BE THAT EVERYONE WHO CALLS ON THE NAME OF THE LORD WILL BE SAVED.' 22 Men of Israel, listen to these words : Jesus the Nazarene, a man attested to you by God with miracles and wonders and signs which God performed through Him in your midst, just as you yourselves know - 23 this Man, delivered over by the predetermined plan and foreknowledge of God, you nailed to a cross by the hands of godless men and put Him to death. 24 But God raised Him up again, putting an end to the agony of death, since it was impossible for Him to be held in its power. 25 For David says of Him, 'I SAW THE LORD ALWAYS IN MY PRESENCE; FOR HE IS AT MY RIGHT HAND, SO THAT I WILL NOT BE SHAKEN. 26 'THEREFORE MY HEART WAS GLAD AND MY TONGUE EXULTED; MOREOVER, MY FLESH ALSO WILL LIVE IN HOPE; 27 BECAUSE YOU WILL NOT ABANDON MY SOUL TO HADES, NOR ALLOW YOUR HOLY ONE TO UNDERGO DECAY. 28 'YOU HAVE MADE KNOWN TO ME THE WAYS OF LIFE; YOU WILL

MAKE ME FULL OF GLADNESS WITH YOUR PRESENCE.'
29 Brethren, I may confidently say to you regarding
the patriarch David that he both died and was
buried, and his tomb is with us to this day. 30 And
so, because he was a prophet and knew that
GOD HAD SWORN TO HIM WITH AN OATH TO SEAT
one OF HIS DESCENDANTS ON HIS THRONE, 31 he
looked ahead and spoke of the resurrection of the
Christ, that HE WAS NEITHER ABANDONED TO HADES,
NOR DID His flesh SUFFER DECAY. 32 This Jesus God
raised up again, to which we are all witnesses. 33
Therefore having been exalted to the right hand
of God, and having received from the Father the
promise of the Holy Spirit, He has poured forth this
which you both see and hear. 34 For it was not
David who ascended into heaven, but he himself
says : 'THE LORD SAID TO MY LORD, "SIT AT MY RIGHT
HAND, 35 UNTIL I MAKE YOUR ENEMIES A FOOTSTOOL
FOR YOUR FEET."' 36 Therefore let all the house of
Israel know for certain that God has made Him both
Lord and Christ -this Jesus whom you crucified."

The Ingathering

37 Now when they heard this, they were pierced
to the heart, and said to Peter and the rest of
the apostles, "Brethren, what shall we do?" 38
Peter said to them, "Repent, and each of you
be baptized in the name of Jesus Christ for the
forgiveness of your sins; and you will receive the
gift of the Holy Spirit. 39 For the promise is for you
and your children and for all who are far off, as
many as the Lord our God will call to Himself." 40
And with many other words he solemnly testified
and kept on exhorting them, saying, "Be saved
from this perverse generation!" 41 So then, those
who had received his word were baptized; and
that day there were added about three thousand
souls. 42 They were continually devoting themselves
to the apostles' teaching and to fellowship, to the
breaking of bread and to prayer. 43 Everyone kept
feeling a sense of awe; and many wonders and

signs were taking place through the apostles. 44 And all those who had believed were together and had all things in common; 45 and they began selling their property and possessions and were sharing them with all, as anyone might have need. 46 Day by day continuing with one mind in the temple, and breaking bread from house to house, they were taking their meals together with gladness and sincerity of heart, 47 praising God and having favor with all the people. And the Lord was adding to their number day by day those who were being saved.

Acts Two	Scroll of Esther and Joseph
Spoke with other tongues	The decrees were sent out in all the languages of the provinces; Joseph concealed that he understood Hebrew.
The Spirit gave them utterance	Esther was a symbol of the Holy Spirit working in the life of her husband to save the Jews.
"YOU WILL NOT ABANDON MY SOUL TO HADES, NOR ALLOW YOUR HOLY ONE TO UNDERGO DECAY"	The jealousy of the Bridegroom did not allow Israel or Esther to remain in captivity to and subject to death plans.

ABOUT THE AUTHOR

Dr. Hollisa Alewine has her B.S. and M.Ed. from Texas A&M and a Doctorate from Oxford Graduate School; she is the author of Standing with Israel: A House of Prayer for All Nations, The Creation Gospel Bible study series, and a programmer on Hebraic Roots Network. Dr. Alewine is a student and teacher of the Word of God.

OTHER BOOKS IN THIS SERIES

BE KY

www.bekybooks.com